漢字說

UNDERSTANDING

CHINESE CHARACTERS VIA GRAPHS
AND PICTURES

浦寅 著

老浦，汉字文化学者，资深媒体人，汉字创意艺术家

Mr. Pu Yin, a Chinese specialist in culture,
a senior social media specialist, and an artist on creative Chinese characters.

作者简介

浦寅的身份总是在变化，毕业于北京师范大学中文系，当过警察、教师、大型国企老总秘书、高新企业高管、私营企业老板、境外媒体国内高管等等，期间还曾辞去一切公职在家读书三年。

丰富的阅历和庞杂的知识成就了浦寅从事一个新鲜的行业：职业电视节目策划人。不从属于任何单位，像一个游方郎中，穿梭于京城各大媒体，策划各类电视节目。先后担任凤凰卫视《一虎一席谈》制片人，央视《艺术人生》总策划，北京电视台《五星夜话》《有话就说》总策划，央视《夜线》《第十演播室》总策划。并在央视、新华社、北京电视台、多个地方卫视的电视栏目，以及中央人民广播电台、中国国际广播电台担任文化评论员。

现场用毛笔书写汉字，用汉字的寓意解释、评论社会热点，是老浦文化点评的一大特色。

自媒体时代，老浦拿起毛笔，在自家书房录制自媒体视频《老浦识字》，每期讲解一个汉字，致力于用传统文化的视角，洞悉当代的社会万象。

2013年10月，在新华社手机电视台创办《老浦拆字评天下》，每期通过一个汉字评论社会热点。

2015年1月，用同样的方法，在中央人民广播电台文艺之声，每天用一个汉字评论文艺新闻。

作为受到传统文化多年熏陶，同时具有很强当代意识的文化学者，老浦在传统书法的基础上，根据汉字甲骨文、金文的造型，开发了自己独特的汉字创意作品。这样的艺术创作还得到了国际艺术大师周氏山作的悉心指点。

2014年4月17日，浦寅应邀前往联合国日内瓦总部，举办了为期15天的《画说汉字》象形文字展览。这个展览是2014年联合国中文日的主要活动，共展出浦寅象形文字创意作品60幅，联合国代理总干事穆勒出席开幕式，对作品给予了高度评价。

2014年11月，浦寅在北京中外首工美术馆举办了《汉字的魅力》汉字创意作品展，展出新作100幅，获得各方好评，许多家长带孩子前来接受传统文化熏陶，展览中多幅作品被藏家收藏。

2017年2月13日，浦寅在"得到"APP上的专栏《老浦识字》上线，受到热烈欢迎。

ABOUT THE AUTHOR

Pu Yin, graduated from the Department of Chinese, Beijing Normal University, employed as police officer, teacher, secretary of China's giant state-owned enterprise, senior executive, managing director of private company, chief representative of foreign media and others. He also read a full-time three-year course.

Rich experiences and a wide variety of knowledge contribute Mr. Pu Ying to be in a new position- a professional TV programmer. He has not been titled by any particular institution but commissioning projects for major media in Beijing. He was employed as a producer in a talk show called "Yihu Yixi Tan" produced by Phoenix Satellite TV, executive director of "Drawn to Life", "Nightline", "The Tenth Studio", which are the interviews programmes by CCTV, and also acts as programmer of two TV programmes produced by BTV, called "Wuxing Yehua" and "Youhua Jiushuo", respectively. And he serves as cultural analyst for CCTV, News Agency, BTV, CNR, CRI and other programmes in local Broadcasting Corporation.

Writing Chinese characters with brush, explaining the denotations of the Chinese characters, and commenting on the most-discussed social issues are the characteristics of the cultural comments by Mr. Pu Yin.

In We-media era, Mr. Laopu records the video on calligraphy brush writing in his workroom. The video project is called "Laopu Shizi". In each episode, he devotes to explaining every Chinese character from the perspectives of traditional culture for understanding the contemporary society.

In October 2013, he launched a programme called "Laopu Chaizi Pingtianxia" in Xinhua news agency mobile phone network. In the programme, he comments the social issues upon a single Chinese character.

In January, 2015, he took the same methods to comment on literary news in the programme called "Voice of the Literary", CNR.

Influenced by traditional culture for many years, Mr. Laopu, who is a cultural scholar with strong contemporary consciousness, develops creative works of Chinese characters based on the traditional calligraphy, particularly on the oracle bone inscriptions and Chinese bronze inscriptions. Such works are also instructed by Chinese contemporary artists ShanZuo, the Zhou Brother.

17 April, 2014, Mr. Pu Yin was invited to hold a 15-days exhibition on pictographic characters in Geneva, headquarter of the UN. The topic is "Huashuo Hanzi". That exhibition is one of the major activities in UN Chinese Language Day in 2014. 60 pieces of the creative works are showed and Mueller, temporarily Secretary-General of the United Nations, is warmly invited to attend the closing ceremony. He gives a high appraisal to the works.

In November, 2014, Mr Pu Yin held creative Chinese characters exhibition- "The Charming of the Chinese characters" in Beijing Art Museum. 100 pieces of work are showed and are widely recognized. Parents with their children embraced the Chinese traditional culture. Some of the works were collected by collectors.

In February 13, 2017, column edited by Mr. Pu Yin - "Laopu Shizi" was officially launched and received a warm welcome.

序 言
FOREWORD

序 言

　　中国有一个古老的传说，一个长着四只眼，名叫仓颉的智者创造了汉字。成功之日，天上降下粟米雨，似乎是上天在向人类祝贺，鬼神在夜晚哭泣，似乎对人类掌握文字感到惊恐。这个故事显示了中国人对汉字的敬畏态度，也是联合国选择农历"谷雨"节气举办中文日活动的由来。

　　汉字是目前仍在使用的古老文字，已经有五千多年的历史了。伴随着代代中国人的繁衍，汉字的使用从未中断。直到今天，汉字仍在电脑、手机中被方便地使用，承载着中国文化的过去、现在和未来。

　　汉字是象形文字，中国古代的先民描摹大自然中的山川、草木、动物以及人的形态，创造了最早的汉字，契刻在陶器、龟甲、兽骨上。这里展示的许多古老的汉字，高度简洁明晰，任何人都能够直接辨识。

　　作为人类生活的记录，早期的汉字反映了先民的许多生活图景和精神生活，体现了原始的世界观，对中国文化的形成和发展产生了深远的影响。可以说，汉字是中国文化的基因。

　　由于汉字象形、会意的特点，从一开始，汉字的书写就具有美感。历经数千年，汉字书法成为世界文化艺术中一个独特的艺术门类。人们把善于书写汉字的人称为书法家，伟大的书法家受到人们世世代代的尊崇。儿童从小就练习书法。在中国，人们往往通过观察一个人的汉字书写来评判他的个性和文化修养。

　　今天，汉字不仅在中国越来越受重视，在世界上也引起了人们的广泛兴趣，作为中国文化的源头，汉字是世界了解中国文化的一把钥匙。

　　但是随着电脑的普及，提笔忘字甚至不再用笔写字，几乎成为每个人的常态。不仅如此，原本寓意丰富的汉字原意，大多数人已经不再了解。老浦在手机应用"得到"App 上办了一个付费专栏《老浦识字》，很多用户都是和孩子一起学习。因为在掌握汉字原意的问题上，家长和孩子处在同一条起跑线。经常有小学生用户向老浦报告：这个字的知识已经分享给了爸爸、妈妈、爷爷、奶奶。

　　这本书收集了老浦 2014 年赴联合国举办《画说汉字》展览的主要作品，还收集了一些近期创作的汉字象形创意作品，目的在于用艺术的方式展现汉字甲骨文、金文原意，推广汉字文化。

　　真诚希望这本小册子能够帮助您打开汉字之门，了解汉字，喜爱汉字。

FOREWORD

A Chinese legend goes that Chinese characters were invented by Cang Jie. The legend relates that on the day the characters were created, people saw crops falling like rain, as if sending a note of congratulation, whereas heard ghosts wailing, as if the ghosts are frightened by the creations. This legend mirrors the Chinese people's reverence for their language. No wonder that the United Nations close to celebrate Chinese Language Day on 'Grain Rain' day (a season division point in traditional Chinese calendar).

Chinese language can be dated back to more than 5,000 years ago. By virtue of their widespread current use in computers, cellphones, Chinese characters are among the most widely adopted writing system. It can be regarded as the epitome of the past, present and the future of the Chinese culture.

Chinese characters, represent words of language, were originally pictograms, which depicted the objects denoted. Characters derive from pictures of the objects e.g. mountains and hills, animals and plants. Chinese characters, in English, they are sometimes called Han characters, are the oldest continuously used system of writing in the world, and are carved on onto potteries, tortoise shell, and oracle bone. Ancient Chinese characters showed here are simplified and stylized to make anyone easier to understand.

Chinese characters in early stage show the picture of the spiritual world and daily life of Chinese progenitors, and reflect their world views, which heavily impact on the formation and development of Chinese culture. It can be symbolically said that Han characters are the genes of the traditional culture.

Given the hieroglyphic and ideographic semantic features of Chinese characters, the writing of the Chinese language has ever been considered as an aesthetic experience. Over the past thousands of years, Chinese calligraphy has evolved into an unique genre in the world arts and cultures. People who are specialized in written Chinese calligraphy are called skilled calligrapher. Great calligraphers would receive respects from generation to generation. Children are tend to practice calligraphy by copying works. In China, the writing of the Chinese characters can be take as the ways to understand one's self-cultivation and personality.

At present, Han characters not only have been paid much attentions than ever before, but also arouse sweeping interests from the rest of the world. It has been an important key for the world to understand Chinese culture.

However, there are cases that people usually forget how to write a character when they pick up the pen. More than that, many people do not understand the denotations of Chinese characters. Mr. Laopu starts a paid column "Laopu Shizi"on mobile application called "Iget". Many parents and their children are the users of that application.

Parents know the denotations of Han characters as little as their children. Some children write comments on the application saying that they have spread the knowledge to their families.

Mr. Laopu successfully hold an exhibition in UN on the topic of Understanding Chinese Characters via Graphs and Pictures in 2014. The book collects the major works that are showed in that exhibition, and also includes some creative pictograms by Mr. Laopu in recent. The book is for showing oracle bone scripts in artist ways, Chinese bronze inscriptions, and promoting the culture of Chinese characters.

We sincerely expect that this brochure could help you to know the Han characters first, then to understand and even love the Chinese traditional characters.

目录 CONTENTS

015 象形字
THE PICTOGRAPHIC CHARACTER

067 会意字
IDEOGRAPHIC CHARACTERS

139 主题字组
COMPOSITE WORDS

151 叠加字
COMPOUND IDEOGRAPHS (IDENTIEAL COMPONENTS)

171 十二生肖
TWELVE ZODIAC SIGNS

197 吉祥字
AUSPICIOUS WORDS

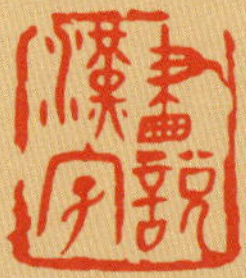
畫說漢字

象形字

THE
PICTOGRAPHIC
CHARACTER

天 HEAVEN

材质：纸质
规格：69.5 × 46.5 cm

Material: paper
Height 69 × width 48 cm

天是中国人"天人合一"观念的直接诠释。大是正面站立的人形，是"大"字。口是人头顶上那无边无际的虚空。合在一起，乃是表示人头上虚无飘渺又无所不在的空间。在中国，天是共同的信仰。在官方，皇帝自称天子，君权天授，所以祭天历来是官方最隆重的仪式。在士大夫，天道才是人间正道。在民间，人们都相信有一个无所不在的老天爷，头上三尺有神明。

天

大 直立的人形
口 人頭上那一
圍虛空
展現的天人
合一概念

象形字

地

材质：纸质
规格：65 × 68 cm

EARTH

Material: paper
Height 65 × width 68 cm

地由"土"和"也"构成，也在古文字里是女性生殖器的象形，是古代生殖崇拜的表现。与"土"结合，表示大地繁衍万物的特徵。《易经》说"地势坤，君子以厚德载物"，指的就是大地象母亲一样对所有的生物一视同仁，生养、爱护、包容大地上的一切生物，此谓"厚德"。

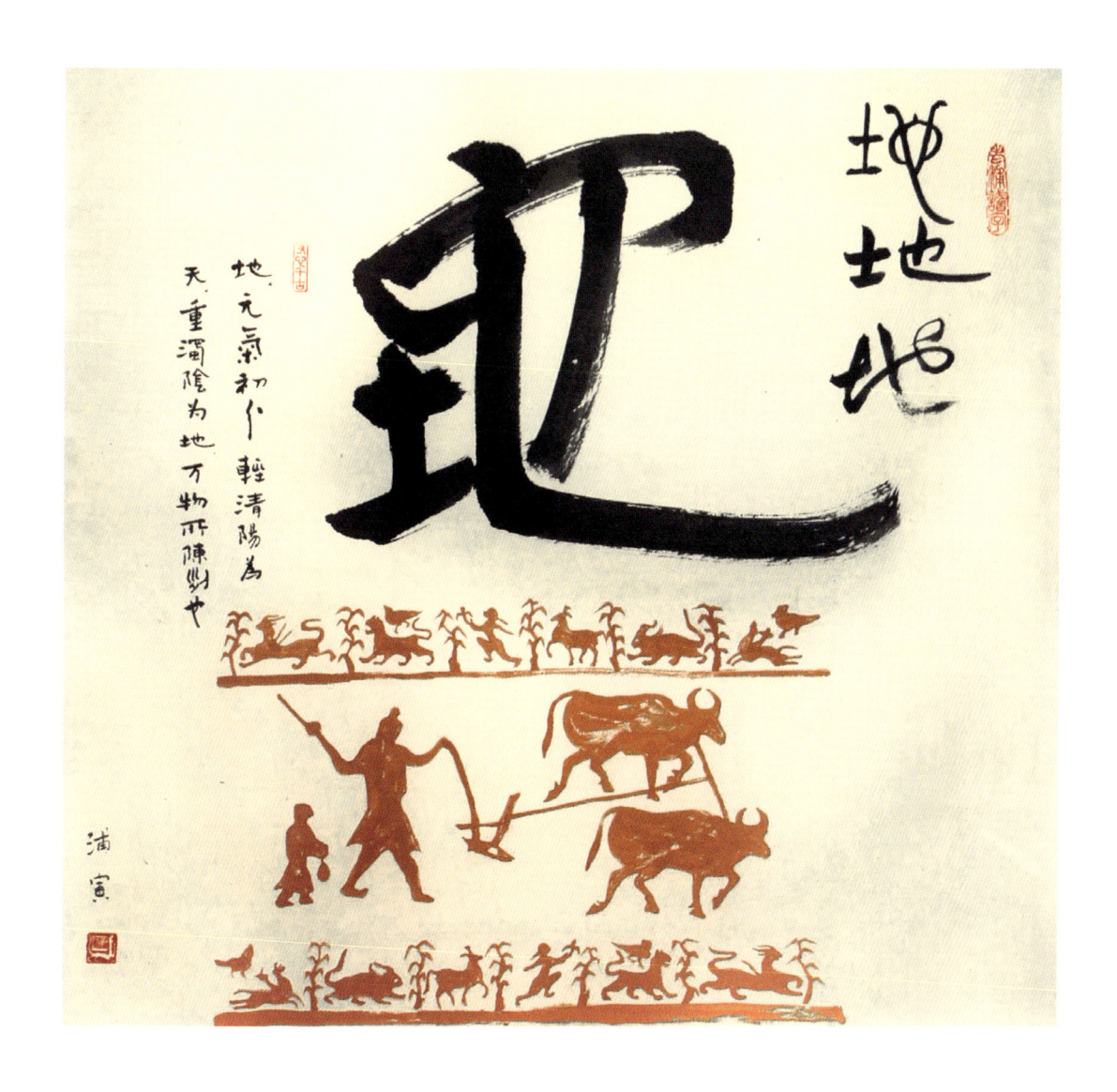

地、元气初分,轻清阳为天,重浊阴为地,万物所陈列也。

象形字

人　　　　PERSON

材质：纸质　　　　Material: paper
规格：69.5 × 46.5 cm　　Height 69.5 × width 46.5 cm

一個躬身垂臂的勞動者，成為"人"，表明古人對人的認識，在於人首先應是動態的生命體。從這個意義而言，動是人的最基本特徵。《說文》曰：人，天地之性最貴者也。在古人眼中，人與天、地同樣重要，被稱為"天、地、人三才"。

象形字　021

大　　　　　　LARGE

材质：纸质　　　　Material: paper
规格：69.5 × 46.5 cm　　Height 69.5 × width 46.5 cm

大象张开双臂双腿正面直立的成年人。《说文》大，天大，地大，人亦大，故大象人形。坦：荡：顶天立地的人，就是大。

大

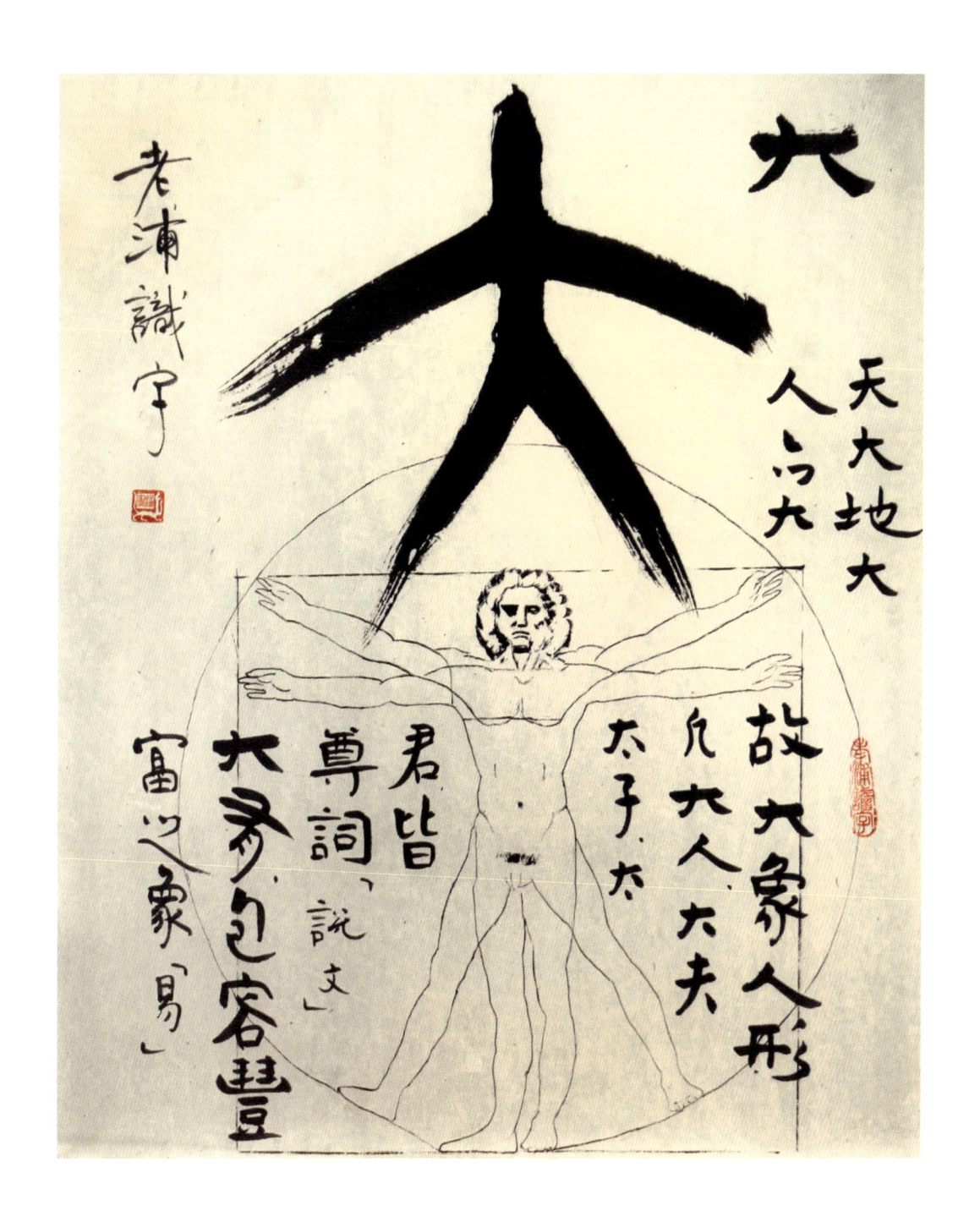

老浦識字

天大地大
人亦大

故大象人形
凡大人大夫
太子、太

君皆尊詞,《說文》
大多包容豐
富之象「易」

象形字 023

男

材质：纸质
规格：69.5 × 46.5 cm

MALE

Material: paper
Height 69.5 × width 46.5 cm

男，甲骨文即，田是农田，丿是力，《徽》男，丈夫也，从田，从力，言男用力於田也，古代男耕女织，力的解读有两种，一种解为犁，为农耕用具，另一种解为右手臂，意为强壮，《说文》力，筋也，象人筋之形，个人感觉手臂的解法靠谱。

象形字

女　　　　　　　FEMALE

材质：纸质　　　　Material: paper
规格：69.5 × 46.5 cm　　Height 69.5 × width 46.5 cm

女．一个敛手端莊跪坐的女人形象．
反映了古人对於一個女人期待：温柔、
安静、從容。

象形字

子   CHILD

材质：纸质
规格：69.5 × 46.5 cm

Material: paper
Height 69.5 × width 46.5 cm

一個幼兒的象形，大腦袋，柔軟的身體，揮舞的手臂象小天使。与子相関的字：孕是胎兒，孳乳是生產。囝包是用布包子。棄去足抛弃此婴。敎是小孩小棍教李孩子。乳是母親哺乳。兒史是小孩囟门尚未長好。等。

象形字 029

好

GOOD

材质：纸质
规格：69.5 × 46.5 cm

Material: paper
Height 69.5 × width 46.5 cm

好。女人和孩子在一起，代表了世界上所有美好的事物。母子关系是人类最真挚、善良和美好的感情。当得上真、善、美。

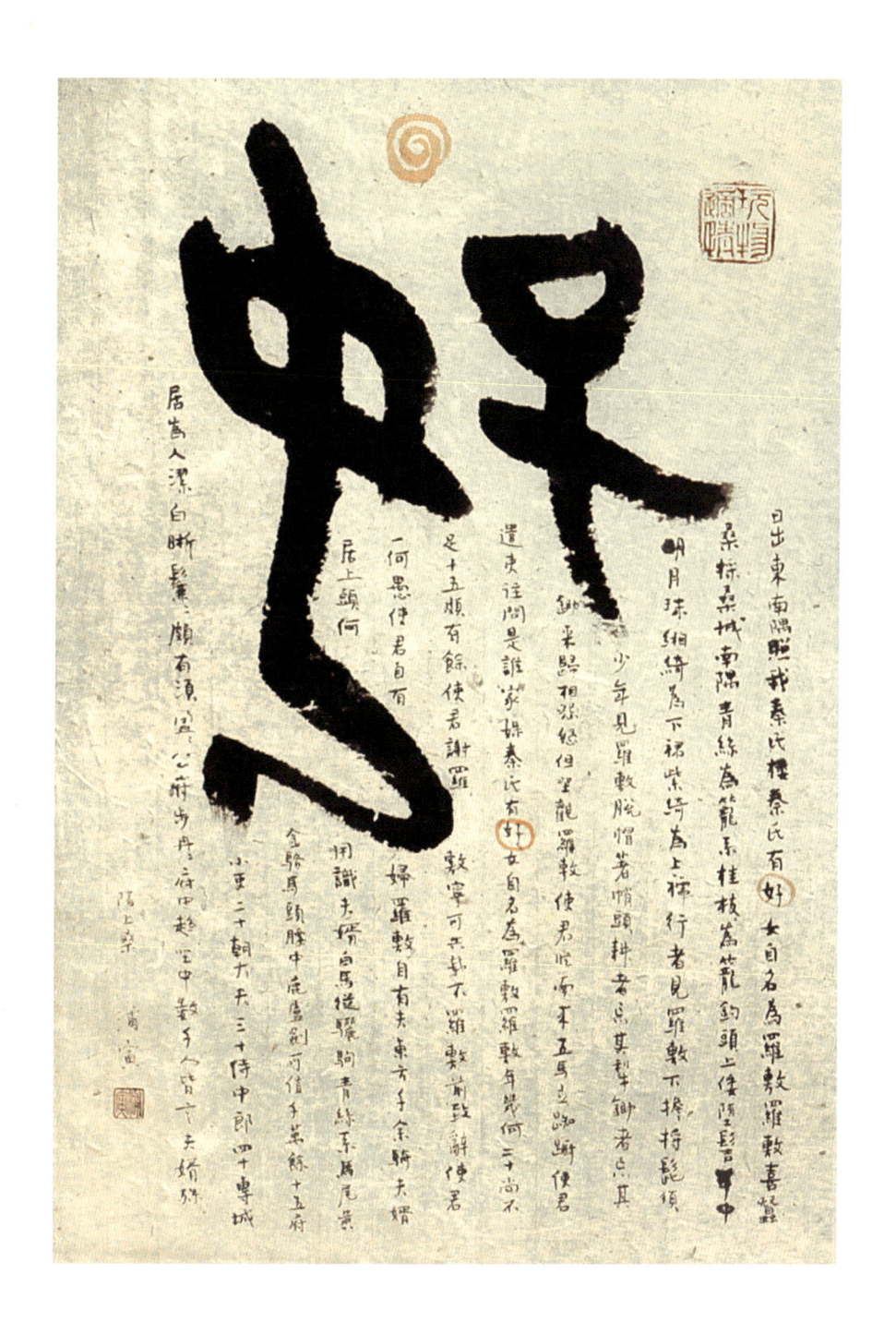

日出東南隅照我秦氏樓秦氏有好女自名為羅敷羅敷喜蠶桑採桑城南隅青絲為籠系桂枝為籠鉤頭上倭墮髻耳中明月珠緗綺為下裙紫綺為上襦行者見羅敷下擔捋髭須少年見羅敷脫帽著帩頭耕者忘其犁鋤者忘其鋤來歸相怨怒但坐觀羅敷使君從南來五馬立踟躕使君遣吏往問是誰家姝秦氏有好女自名為羅敷羅敷年幾何二十尚不足十五頗有餘使君謝羅敷寧可共載不羅敷前致辭使君一何愚使君自有婦羅敷自有夫東方千餘騎夫婿居上頭何用識夫婿白馬從驪駒青絲系馬尾黃金絡馬頭腰中鹿盧劍可值千萬餘十五府小吏二十朝大夫三十侍中郎四十專城居為人潔白晢鬑鬑頗有須盈盈公府步冉冉府中趨坐中數千人皆言夫婿殊

陽上桑
蘭茵

儿

BABY

材质：纸质
规格：69.5 × 40 cm

Material: paper
Height 69.5 × width 40 cm

儿．柔软的身體．大之的腦袋．活象年畫中的大頭娃之．另头頂開口．表明這是一個头頂囟门還沒有融長好的婴兒。

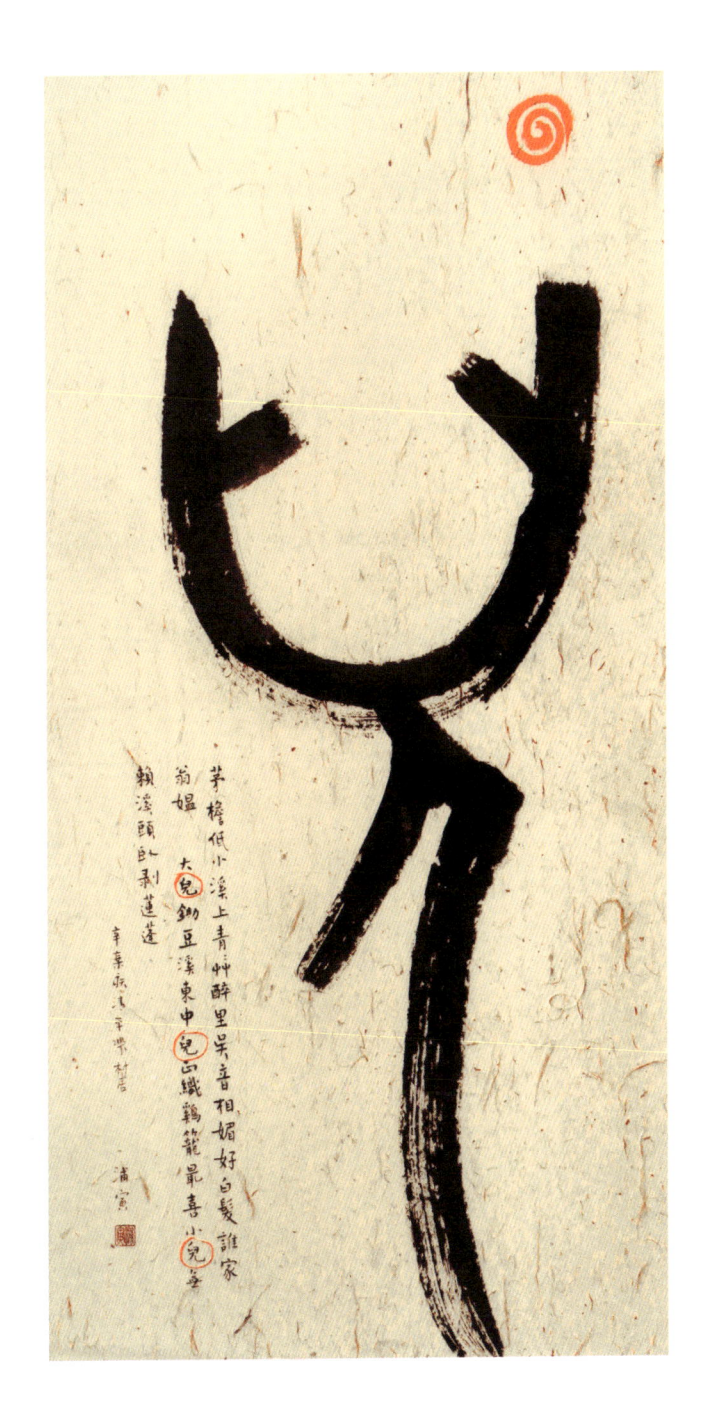

茅檐低小溪上青艸醉里吴音相媚好白髮誰家翁媼 大兒鋤豆溪東中兒正織雞籠最喜小兒亡賴溪頭卧剥蓮蓬

辛亥秋尺子樂齋

浦宴

象形字 033

山　　　MOUNTAIN

材质：纸质
规格：69.5 × 46.5 cm

Material: paper
Height 69.5 × width 46.5 cm

甲骨文山就是山峰轮廓的象形。小篆山规整有美感，但已不是大自然自有山的形象了。中国文化中山具有特殊的意涵。《说文》山，宣也。宣气散，有石而高。山是文人的精神家园。采菊东篱下，悠然见南山。即使身居城市，也要在自家园林中复制出自然山水。

山

象形字　035

水　　　　　　　　WATER

材质：纸质　　　　　Material: paper
规格：69.5 × 46.5 cm　Height 69.5 × width 46.5 cm

甲骨文水像崎岖崖壁飞溅而下的水流，金文水则像一条河流。象形字水抓住了水既可以是一個整體又可以分解為水滴的特徵

水

象形字

日　　　　　　　SUN

材质：纸质　　　　Material: paper
规格：69.5 × 46.5 cm　　Height 69.5 × width 46.5 cm

日是太陽的象形，中間的一點表示光芒。《说文》說曰，太陽之精也。是說日不僅是太陽的形象描摹，還代表太陽的精華。說明古人早就認識到，太陽是有能量的。當然，日在漢語中用的最多的是對時間的表現。"日月盈昃，辰宿列張。

象形字　039

月　　　　　　　MOON

材质：纸质　　　　Material: paper
规格：69.5 × 46.5 cm　　Height 69.5 × width 46.5 cm

☽是月球的象形，有别于☉太阳的恒定。古人用半圆代表月亮。《说文》月，阙也，太阴之精。月亮在夜晚出现，故为阴性。人有悲欢离合，不如意事常八九；月有阴晴圆缺，故成为人生无常、残缺美的代言。

月

见　　　　　　　　　　SEE

材质：纸质　　　　　　Material: paper
规格：69.5 × 40 cm　　Height 69.5 × width 40 cm

見，僅畫一個眼睛代表整個頭部，加上人的身體，就表現出人用眼看見的情景。和卡通的表現方式很相似。在甲骨文中，"見"有好幾種，有站著的，坐著的，還有女人的。在古漢字中，人平視為"見"，仰視為"臣"。

岐王宅里尋常見 崔九堂前幾度聞
正是江南好風景 落花時節又逢君
杜甫詩江南逢李龜年

气

QI

材质：纸质
规格：69.5 × 46.5 cm

Material: paper
Height 69.5 × width 46.5 cm

气《説文》釋为雲气的象形。《禮記·月令》説"天气下降，地气上騰"是説上一横为天气，下一横为地气，中間一横为人气。氣加米表明气是一種象糧食一樣的能量，生命力的象徵。

氣

酒　　　　　LIQUOR

材质：纸质　　　Material: paper
规格：69.5 × 46.5 cm　　Height 69.5 × width 46.5 cm

甲骨文㓰，酒是尖底瓶的酒缸，水旁表示液态。尖底瓶是一种礼器，尖底插入陶琮的中孔，瓶内盛放酒用于祭祀天地。说明酒的最早用途是敬神。西方的酒神精神是自由、艺术和美的代表。中国的酒与诗一起成为放浪形骸的潇洒。

象形字　047

止　　　　　　FOOT

材质：纸质　　　Material: paper
规格：69.5 × 46.5 cm　　Height 69.5 × width 46.5 cm

止是脚掌的剪影，以三趾代表五趾。《说文》止，下基也。象艸木出有址。故以止为足。许慎没见过甲骨文。其实止本身就是足。我们今天常用的停的意思，是引申意。

象形字　049

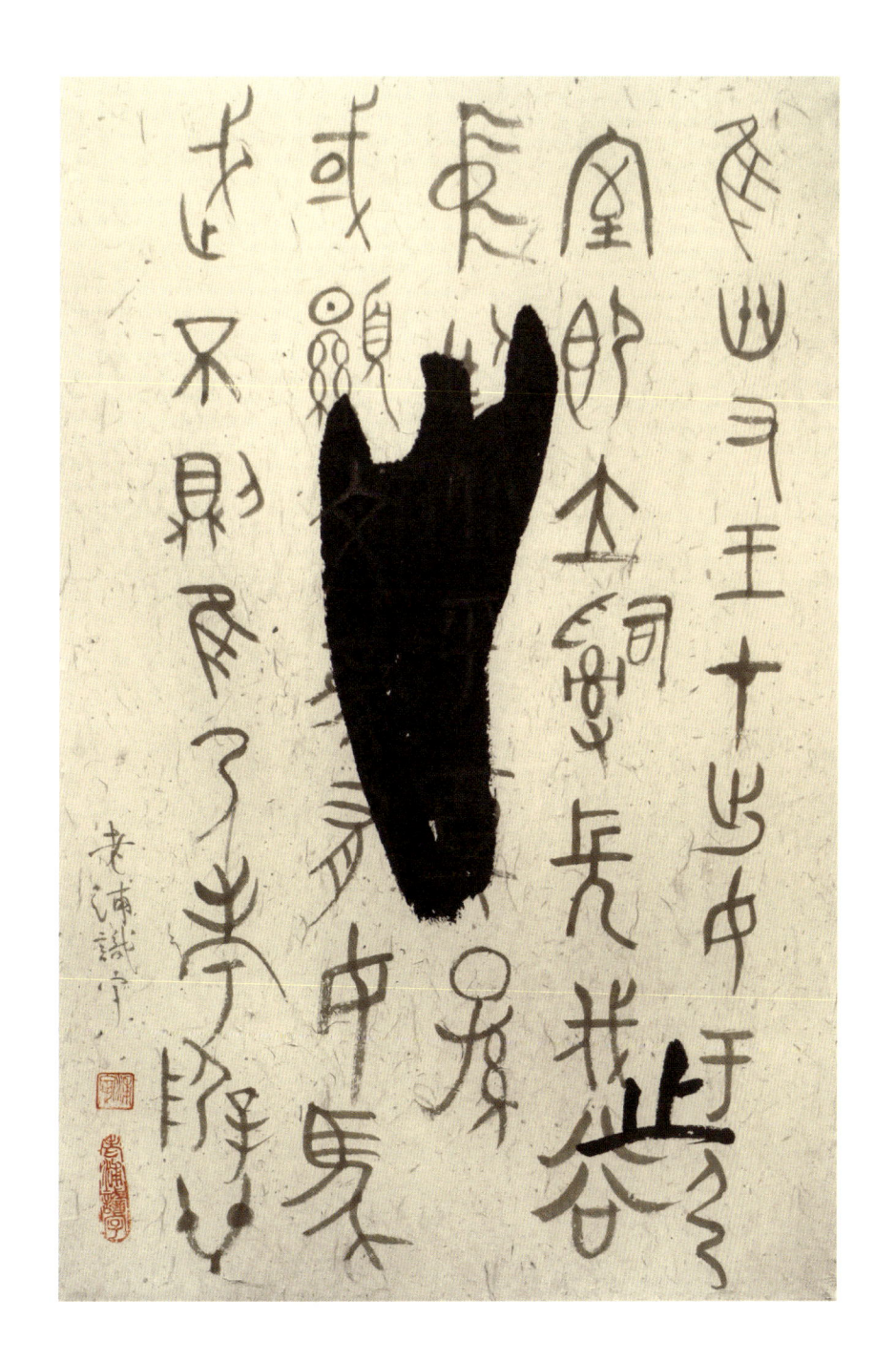

心　　　　　　　　　HEART

材质：纸质　　　　　Material: paper
规格：69.5 × 46.5 cm　Height 69.5 × width 46.5 cm

金文 ⟨⟩ 就是人體心臟的形狀，但中國人從來不認為心臟僅是泵血的器官，而是感知、直覺思考与情感的思維所在，代表人的直覺。

心

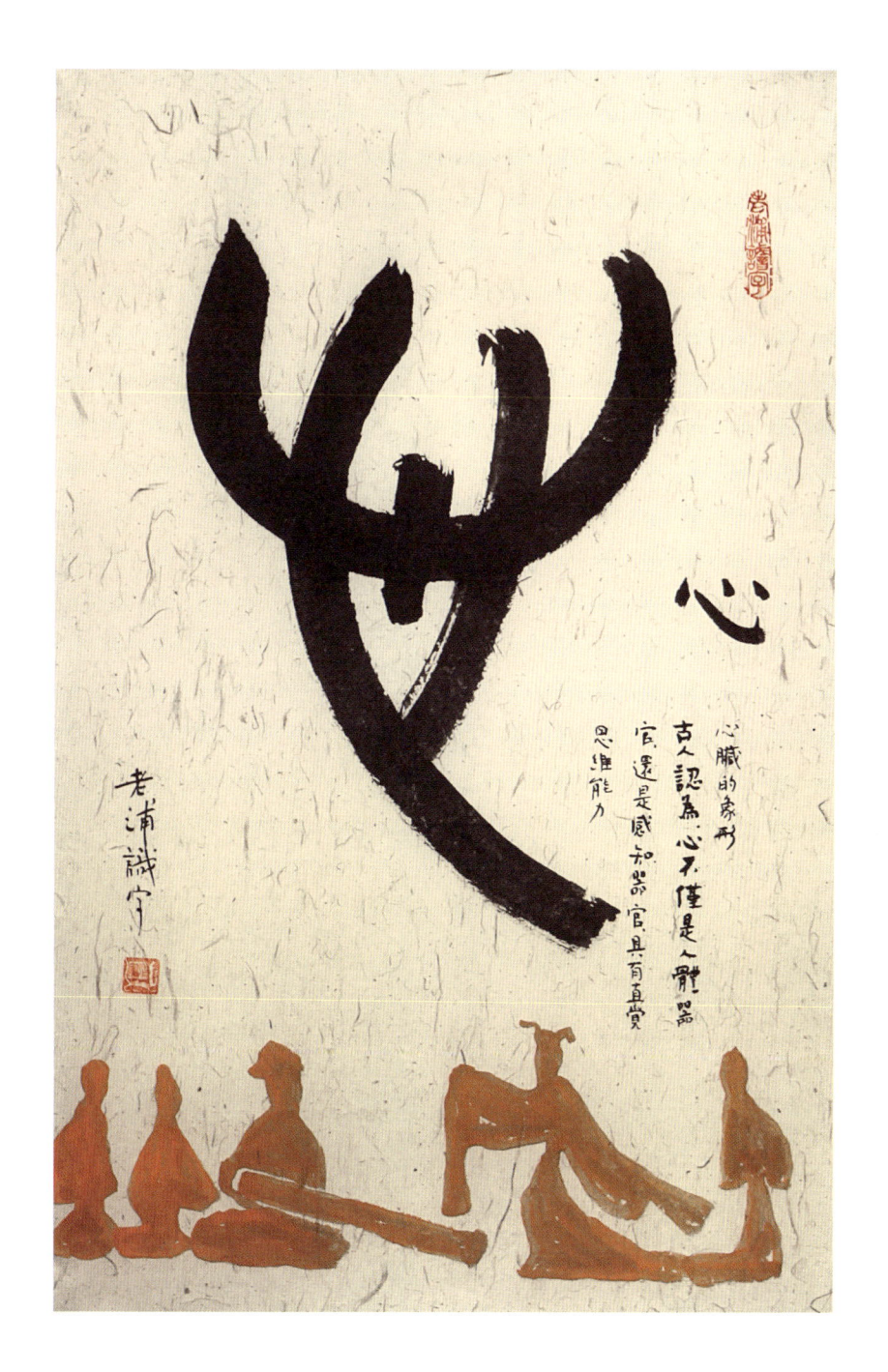

心臟的象形
古人認為心不僅是人體器
官還是感知器官其有直覺
思維能力

老浦識宝

象形字

眉

EYEBROW

材质：纸质
规格：46.5 × 69.5 cm

Material: paper
Height 46.5 × width 69.5 cm

这是一个美女眉眼的象形。迷媚，古人认为一个女人的美在于她的媚力。全在she媚眼之间。正如骆宾王在《讨武曌檄》中说，"掩袖工谗。狐媚偏能惑主"

象形字

车　　VEHICLE

材质：纸质
规格：69.5 × 46.5 cm

Material: paper
Height 69.5 × width 46.5 cm

图中展示的是车的多种写法，可以看出，最早的车是用于战争的。春秋战国时期以战车的数量代指一国的军事实力。千乘之国指有1000辆战车的中等国。

車

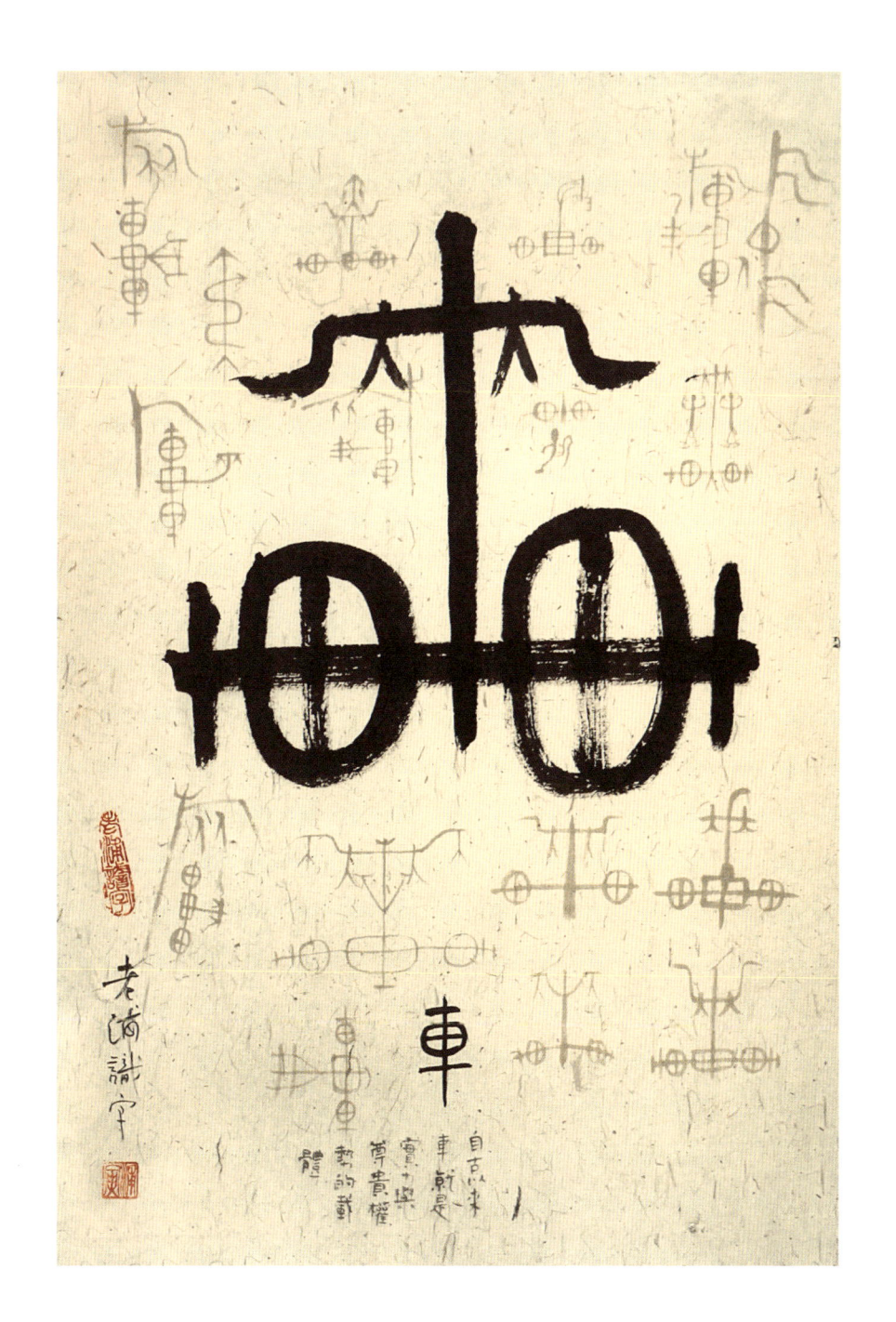

自古以来
車就是
豪华与
尊贵权
势的载
體

象形字

鱼　　　　　　　　FISH

材质：纸质　　　　　Material: paper
规格：69.5 × 46.5 cm　Height 69.5 × width 46.5 cm

鱼：鱼的象形。

鱻：(xiān)，古同鲜。

渔：捕鱼。

象形字　057

鸟

BIRD

材质：纸质
规格：69.5 × 46.5 cm

Material: paper
Height 69.5 × width 46.5 cm

这是长尾鸟的象形，短尾鸟是隹。小篆简化了鸟喙身，但仍是长尾鸟的形象。鸟是商的图腾《史记·殷本纪》"殷契，母曰简狄，为帝喾次妃，行浴见玄鸟堕其卵，简狄取吞之，因孕，生契"契是殷商的始祖。这就是"天命玄鸟，降而生商"。古代民间称男性生殖器为鸟。

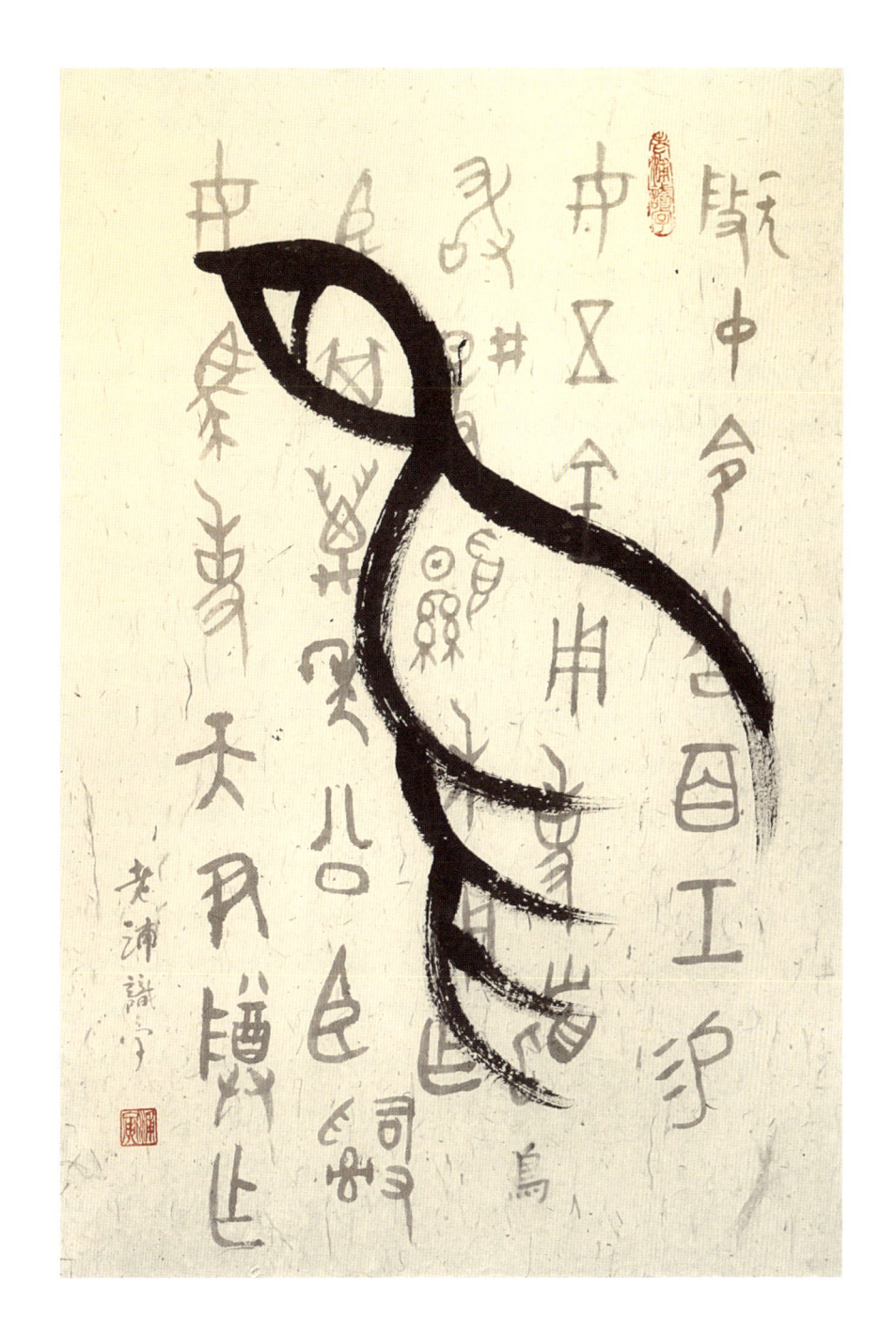

象形字

飞   **FLY**

材质：纸质   Material: paper
规格：69.5 × 46.5 cm   Height 69.5 × width 46.5 cm

籀文飛畫出鳥飛翔的完整形象。篆字飛仍是鳥飛造型，只是更规范了。還有一種寫法乇僅保留雙翅。繁體正書飛仍不失靈動，是最美的漢字之一。

老浦識字

象形字　061

鼎　　　　　DING (RITUAL BRONZE VESSEL)

材质：纸质　　　　Material: paper
规格：69.5 × 46.5 cm　　Height 69.5 × width 46.5 cm

甲骨文 👁 鼎 均显示鼎是有足有耳的青铜容器，祭祀的礼器。《说文》鼎，三足两耳，和五味之宝器也。传说禹铸九鼎，传夏、商、周三代成为政权象征。楚王问鼎大小轻重，有谋权之意，问鼎成为夺取最高政权之意

鼎

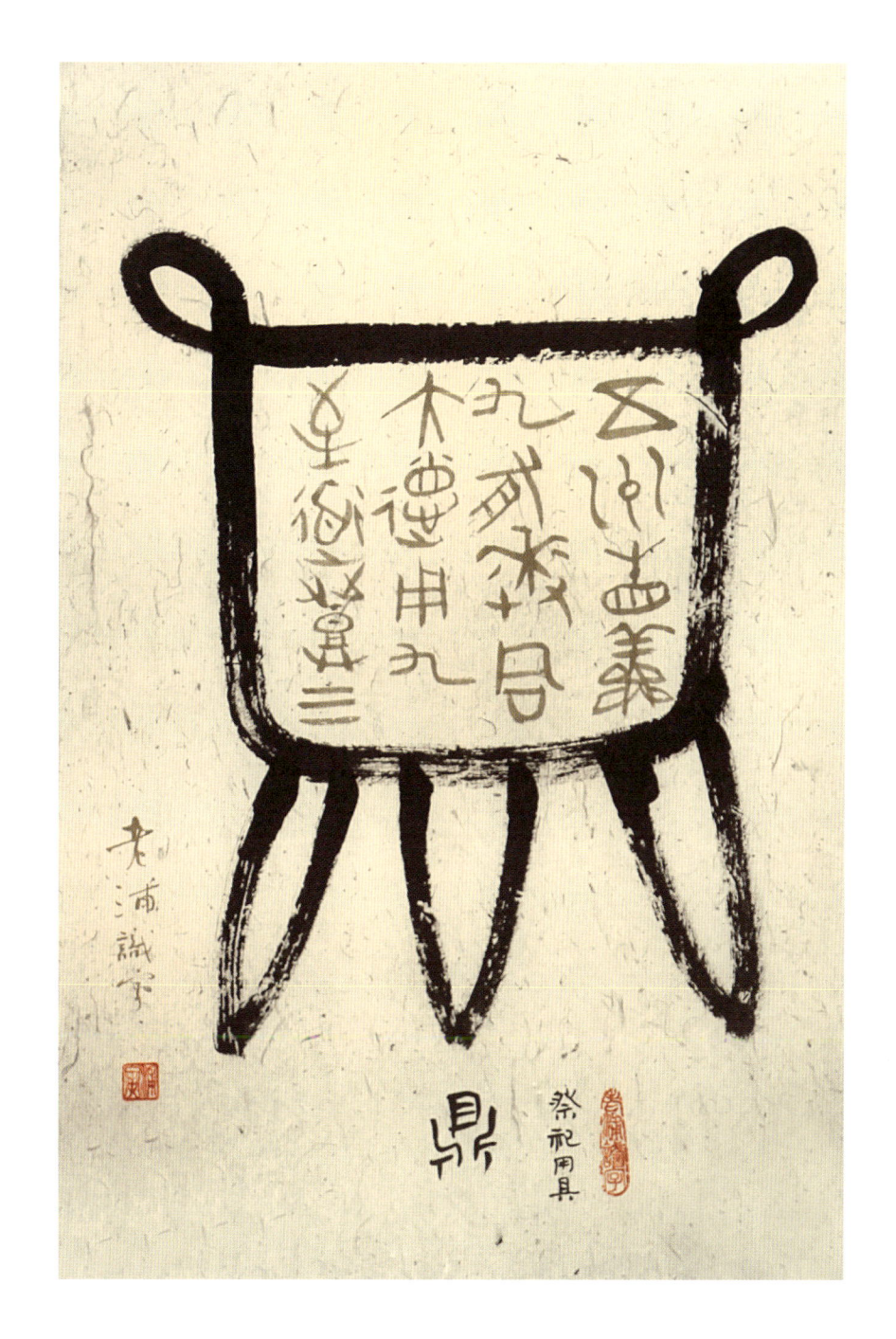

祭祀用具

象形字

皿　BRONZE BOWL

材质：纸质
规格：69.5 × 46.5 cm

Material: paper
Height 69.5 × width 46.5 cm

甲骨文皿是敞口无盖的容器。《说文》皿饭器之用器也。虽然皿是日常生活用具而此多数青铜皿均用于祭祀。由皿构成的字许多与生活有关。如宁，指有屋有皿（饭食）心就安宁。

飲食用器

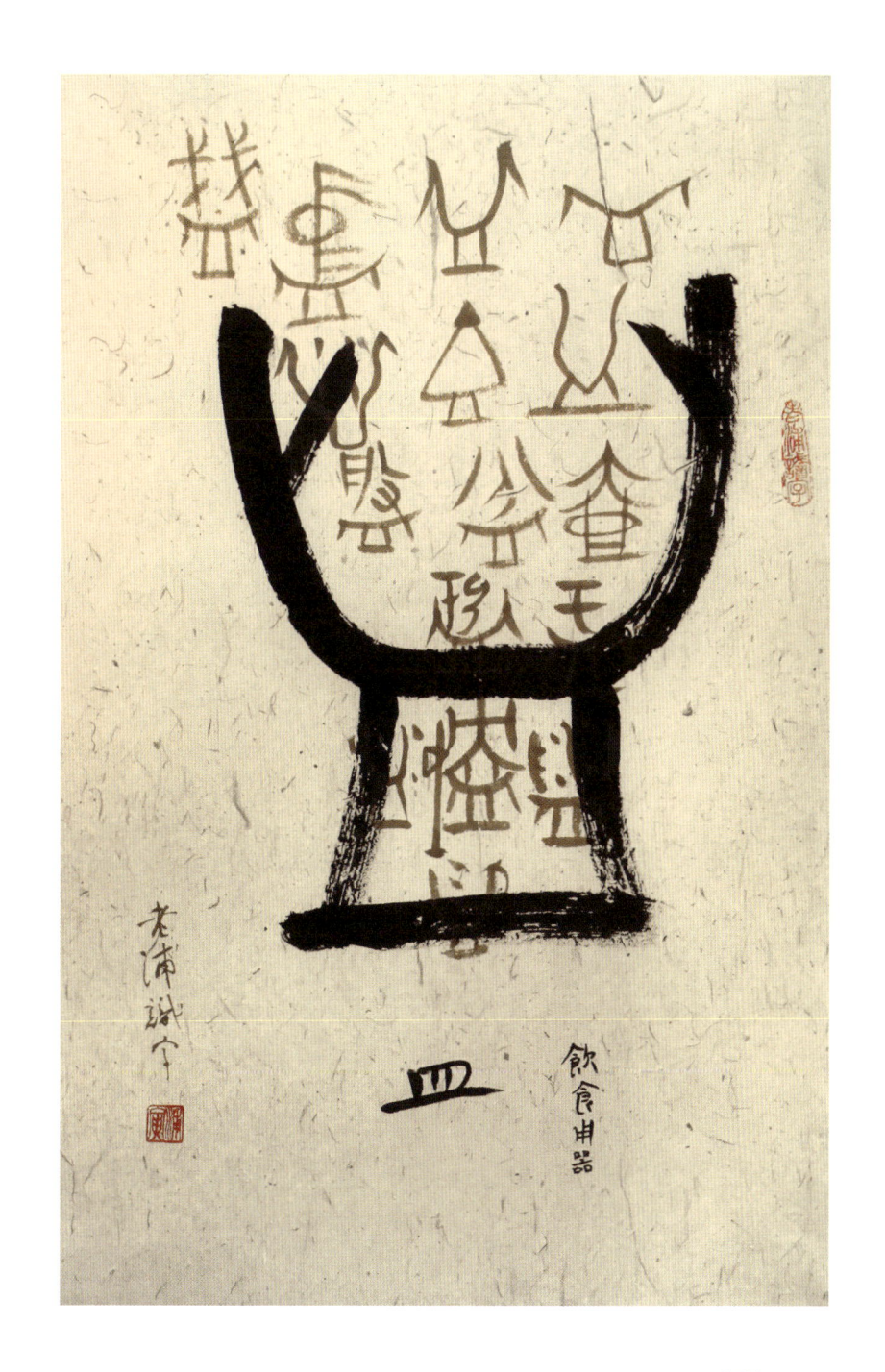

象形字 065

畫說漢字

会意字

IDEOGRAPHIC
CHARACTERS

我   I

材质：纸质
规格：69.5 × 46.5 cm

Material: paper
Height 69.5 × width 46.5 cm

甲骨文 我 是刃部呈锯齿状的兵器，形状巨大威猛。仅用于仪仗以显示威严，成为第一人称，说明"我"的本义是威严、自尊。要取得尊严，首先自己要立得住，自尊自爱。

| 一件仪仗用的兵器 | Ancient weapon held in the hands of a guard of honor |
| 用作第一人称，表示人的本质是尊严，人只有尊重自己才能受人尊敬 | "I" as the first person implies that dignity is the hard-core value of a human. Only those who respect themselves can be respected by others |

辛

這是一件儀仗用的兵器，用作第一人稱表示人的本質是尊嚴，人只有尊重自己才能受人尊敬。

会意字

爱   LOVE

材质：纸质
规格：69.5 × 46.5 cm

Material: paper
Height 69.5 × width 46.5 cm

金文愛多欠，一個人張嘴呵氣或訴說。
女心表示与心情有关，後篆文壽加夊止，
表示捧心走來訴說，豐富了愛的含義，愛
不僅要訴說表達，還要付諸行動。

	表示说出	Speaking out
	双手捧着状	Cupping of two hands
	表示心	A heart
	一个人向另一个人走近	One person approaches another person
	男女二人双手捧心诉说爱意，爱的本质是奉献真心	A man and a woman express mutual affections while holding his/her heart in cupped hands. The nature of love can be boiled down to the revelation of true heart

雙手捧心
也來訴說
愛意，古文
"愛"告訴我
們愛的本
質只奉
獻真心

会意字 071

美

BEAUTY

材质：纸质
规格：70 × 70 cm

Material: paper
Height 70 × width 70 cm

美由 艹羊 和正面直立的人形 大 组成，是一个戴羊首面具祭天舞者的形象。这个健壮、真诚、与神相通的人，是代表美的。大而舒展、匀称，也是美的特征。

羊

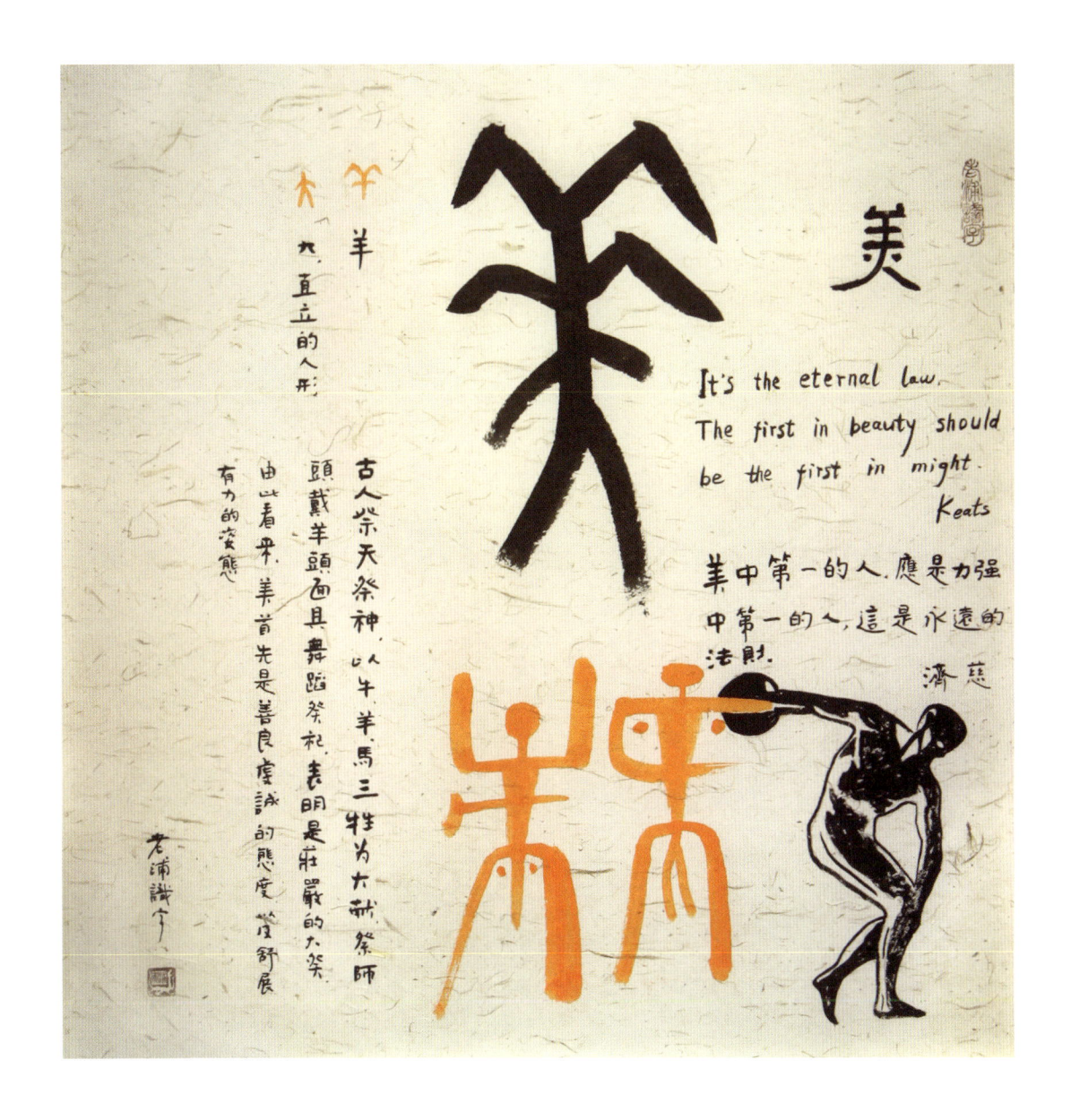

大 直立的人形

美

It's the eternal law.
The first in beauty should
be the first in might.
　　　　　　Keats

美中第一的人，應是力强
中第一的人，這是永遠的
法則。
　　　　　濟慈

古人祭天祭神，以牛羊馬三牲为太牢祭師
頭戴羊頭面具舞蹈祭祝表明是莊嚴的大笑
由此看來，美首先是善良虔誠的態度並舒展
有力的姿態

老浦識字

会意字　073

正   UPRIGHT

材质：纸质
规格：69.5 × 46.5 cm

Material: paper
Height 69.5 × width 46.5 cm

甲骨文由口代表村邑，有围栏的部落，以脚趾代表行进，表示向村邑进发，是征的原字。正是一种动态，要不断调整脚步才能到达目的，没有谁永远正确。

	目标	The goal
	脚趾，表示向目标进发	Toes, meaning heading toward goal
	是直达目标的行为，脚跟的行进表示为达目标需要不断调整	"Upright" represents a behavior leading directly toward the goal. The toe movement denotes continual adjustment till attainment of the goal

会意字

此．表示目標
ㄣ．腳趾表示舉
步向目標進发
正是直達目標的
行為，腳趾的行
進表示為達
目標需不斷
調整

会意字　075

孝　　　　　　　FILIAL PIETY

材质：纸质 / 竹简　　Material: paper / bamboo slips
规格：71 × 46.5 cm　Height 71 × width 46.5 cm

孝，是长髮老人"耂"和孩子"子"组成，表示孩子与老人在一起。含饴弄孙是老年人最大的乐趣，所以孝的本意是陪伴。

孝 孝 孝

游問孝子曰今之孝者是謂
能養至於犬馬皆能有養
不敬何以別乎
《論語》

子游問孝子曰今之孝者是謂能養至於犬馬皆能有養不敬何以別乎

孝浦說文

孝 長髮老者
早文章後代
原意為孫攙扶老人
父兮生我
母兮鞠我
拊我畜我
長我育我
顧我復我
出入腹我
欲報之德
昊天罔極
《詩經》

勇   COURAGE

材质：纸质 / 竹简　　Material: paper / bamboo slips
规格：46.5 × 71 cm　　Height 46.5 × width 71 cm

勇，甬是通的意思，而力又是犁铧的象形。用犁铧耕耘土地，使其通畅，反映了农业社会朴素的思维。而"狭路相逢勇者胜"更是发力通路的完美解释。

狭路相逢勇者胜

乙未冬 浦寅

会意字　079

铁　　　　　　　IRON

材质：纸质 / 竹简　　Material: paper / bamboo slips
规格：46.5 × 71 cm　Height 46.5 × width 71 cm

铁，金字旁，一個矢，這是一支拴着一根絲綫的箭，是专门射飞禽的。射中以後顺着絲綫可以顺利找到獵物。鐵這漢字反映了古人對這種金屬的認識：不僅堅硬，而且鋒利。

鐵

鐵馬入河入夢來

会意字 081

思　　　　THOUGHT / THINKING

材质：纸质　　　　Material: paper
规格：71 × 46.5 cm　　　　Height 71 × width 46.5 cm

思由囟（囟门，代表大脑）和心（心脏，代表心灵）组成。用大脑思考，代表逻辑思维。用心灵感受代表直觉和感情。这是东方的思维特征。不仅注重理性思考，同时注重心灵感受。正如《道德经》"道可道非常道"，大道靠感受，不能清晰言说。

	婴儿的头，指人的大脑	A baby's head, referring to human brain
	人的心	Human heart
	在中国人看来，大脑和心都是思维的器官，大脑的思考代表理性，心的感知代表感性。东方的智慧是两者的配合	In the view of the Chinese people, both the brain and heart are organs for thought, with the first representative of rationality, and the latter of perceptiveness. The oriental wisdom should combine both

囟 囟

心 心

囟 像兒兒頭部俯視圖，代指人的大腦

心 心代指人的心臟

在中國人看來，大腦和心臟都是思維的器官。囟(大腦)的思考代表理性，心的感知代表感性，而于智慧是兩者的匯合。

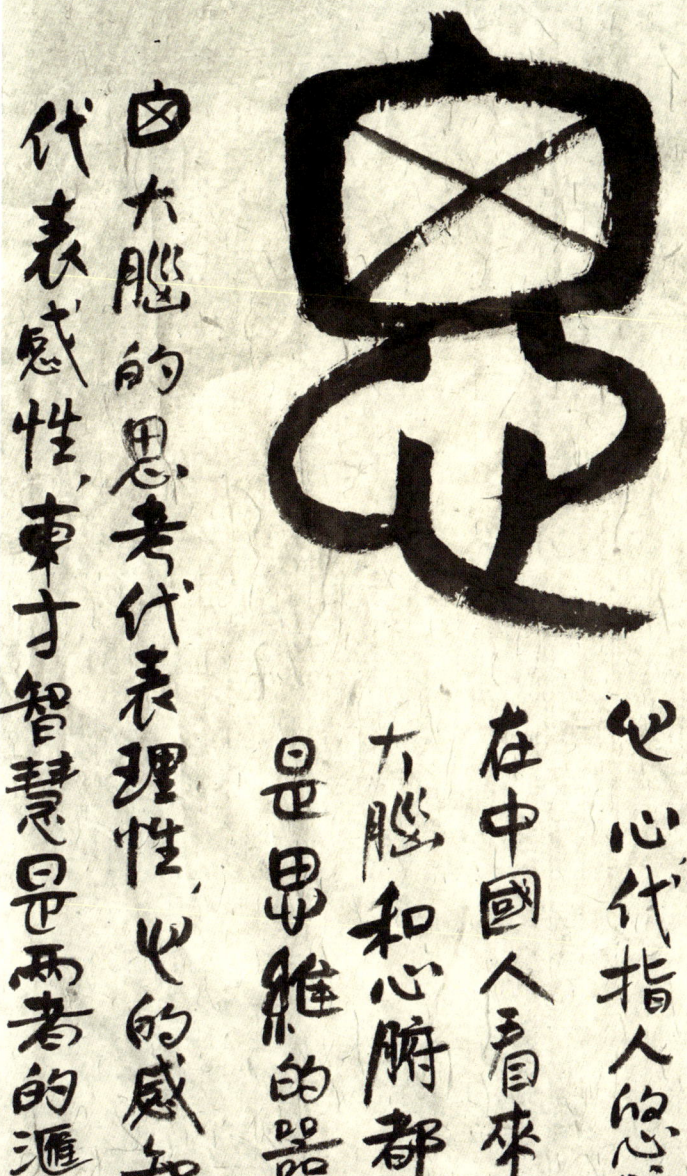

保　　　　　　**PROTECT / PROTECTION**

材质：纸质　　　　Material: paper
规格：71 × 46.5 cm　　Height 71 × width 46.5 cm

甲骨文㺇是一人㐁反抱一子㝍，表示保护孩子。金文㒨延袭了甲骨文字型。缘于古人外出，须将孩子背在背上方保安全。金文㒨改为正面抱子保护，意义更加清晰。篆文保已经看不出原意了。

	婴儿	A baby
	成年人怀抱或背负状	An adult's holding a baby in her arms or carrying it on her back
	母亲把不会行走的婴儿抱在胸前 原意为保护、抚养	A mother holds her reclining baby in both arms. "Protection" originally means guarding and nurturing

084　　会意字

保 子 柔弱的嬰兒 子 一個成人懷抱

或背負状。

柔弱的嬰女兒不能行走，母親需要時：把孩子抱在胸前。保原意為保抱、撫養。

人類就是在這樣溫暖懷抱生生不息

会意字　085

望　　　　　　LOOK AT

材质：纸质
规格：71 × 46.5 cm

Material: paper
Height 71 × width 46.5 cm

床前明月光，疑是地上霜。
举头望山月，低头思故乡。
李白这首诗正是"望"这个汉字的
形象写照。一个人站在高高的土堆
上，用一个大大的眼睛代替整个
头部表示他用眼张望，而远方
那一轮明月，让这个汉字自
带满满的诗意。

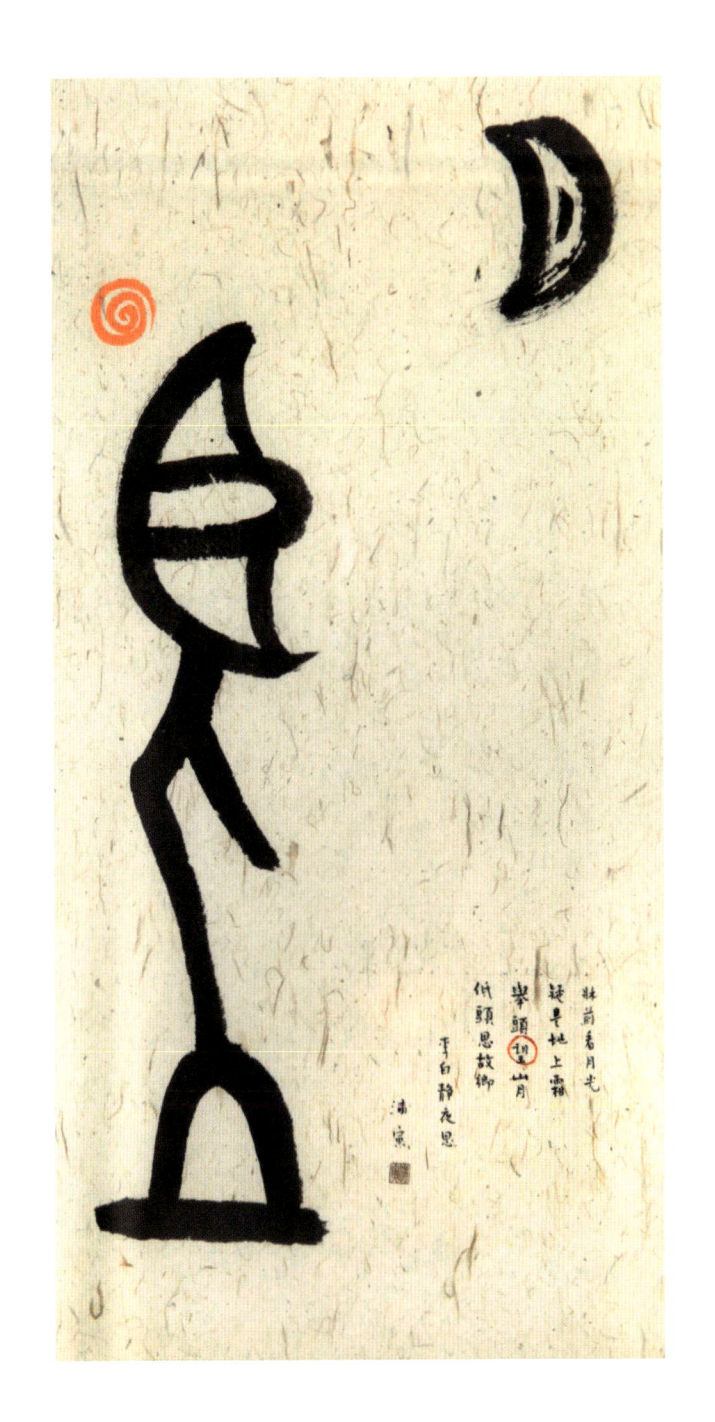

床前看月光
疑是地上霜
举头望山月
低头思故乡

李白 静夜思

会意字　087

家　　　　　　　　HOME

材质：纸质　　　　　Material: paper
规格：71 × 46.5 cm　Height 71 × width 46.5 cm

家是房屋门里的一头猪，而且有的甲骨文还特意标明是一头公猪。猪是人类由游猎采集向农业定居的产物。养猪意味着定居、安宁的生活。所以用屋里养猪代表家庭。公猪则象征开枝散叶、繁衍生息。

	房屋	A house
	公猪	A boar
	房屋里养猪是从游猎转向定居的标志，一头公的种猪代表着一群猪，家里有猪也是富裕的象征。猪的性情温和，表示家庭生活以和睦为宗旨	Indoor pig-raising symbolizes the transition from nomadic to settled life. A boar inside the house becomes a sign of wealth as it can bring to life a herd of swine. In light of its mild character. A pig reflects the orientation of family life toward peace and harmony

宀 房屋 豕 一隻 宀 豬 房屋裡養

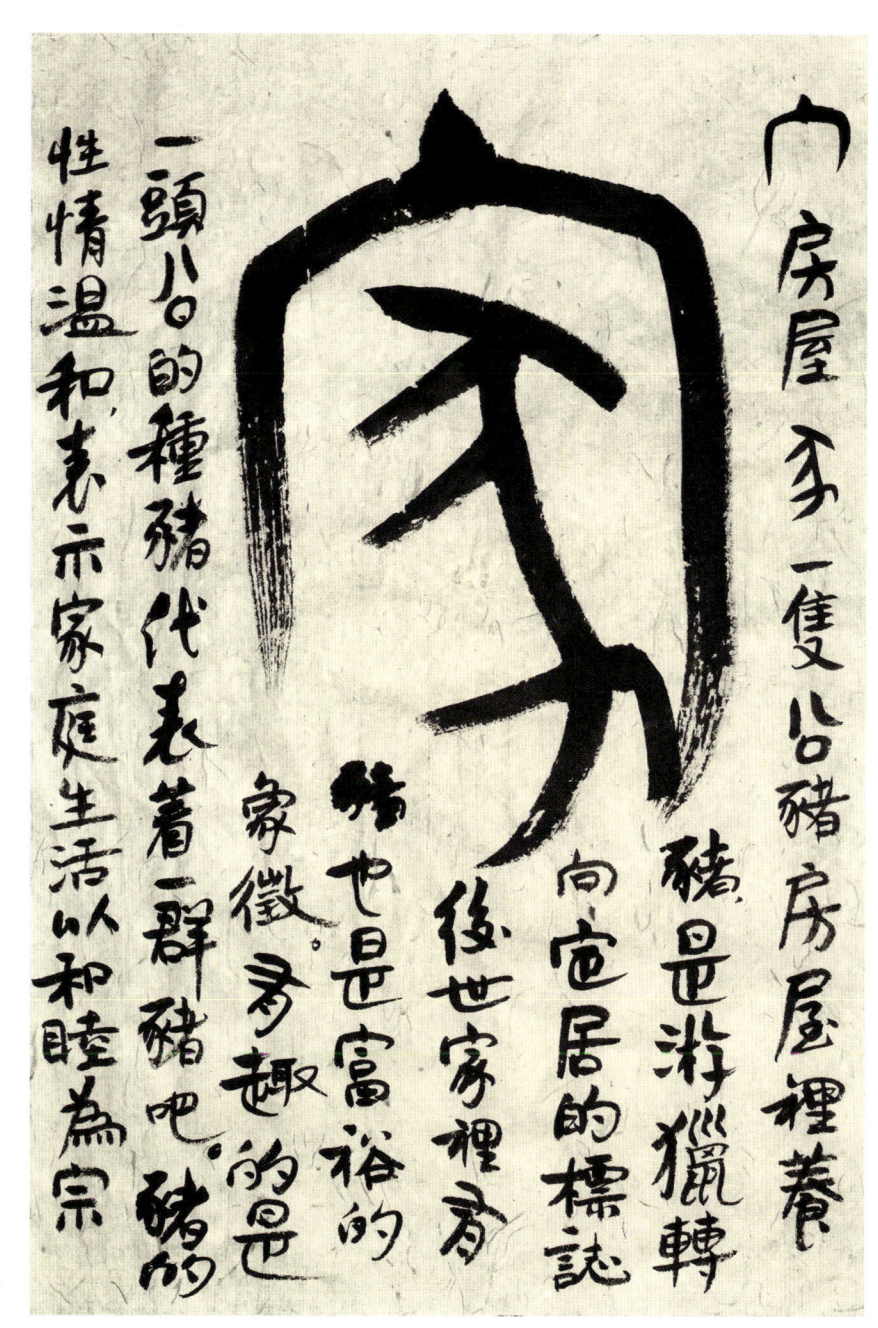

豬，是游獵轉向宜居的標誌，後世家裡有豬也是富裕的家徵，多麼有趣的是一頭肥的種豬代表著一群豬吧，豬的性情溫和，表示家庭生活以和睦為宗

道　　　　　TAO

材质：纸质　　　　Material: paper
规格：71 × 46.5 cm　　Height 71 × width 46.5 cm

甲骨文 𰀀 從彳行，表示道路，十字路口。屮，止，一隻脚表示行走。金文 𰀁 從彳從首。首，人的頭部。寸，手，表示這裏可以看清人的面目的寬廣大路，加手則成爲"導"字的原型道後引申爲普遍真理。"一陰一陽之謂道"。立天之道，曰陰與陽；立地之道，曰柔與剛；立人之道，曰仁與義。

	道路	A road
	头脑	Brain
	行走	Walking
	不但是道路，在中国哲学中还表示终极道理	The "way" means more than the road, but the ultimate truth in the Chinese philosophy

道在中國哲學中表示終極真理，既是道路也是道理

行表示道路
首表示頭腦
彳表示行走

会意字 091

德　　　VIRTUE

材质：纸质　　　Material: paper
规划：71 × 46.5 cm　　　Height 71 × width 46.5 cm

甲骨文德，彳表示道路，由表示眼睛直视前方，不偏离道路。金文德下面加心，表示与人的心灵有关。德的本意是行坦荡大道，正直无私。

彳	道路	A road
由	眼睛上有一条直线，表示一直向前	A straight line above the eye, meaning going straight forward
心	正直的心态	Integrity
德	意思为不走小路或不走近路	"Virtue" means avoiding bypasses or shortcuts
德	是中国文化的核心概念，是勤劳朴实、仗义果敢、居安思危、善始善终	"Virtue" as a core concept of the Chinese culture is a collage of different meanings of industry, plainness, just, resolution, vision, caution, perseverance and consistency

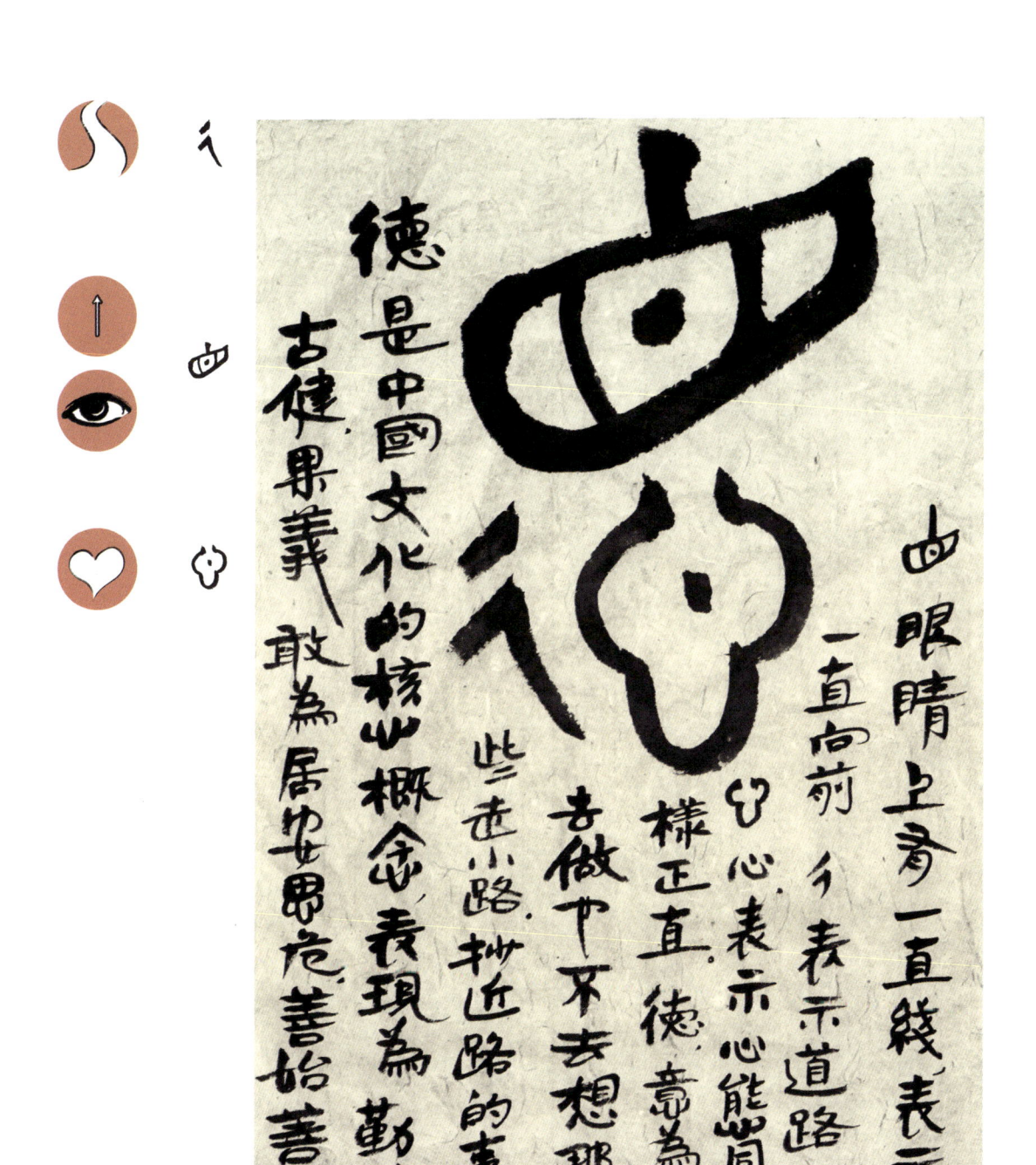

德是中國文化的核心概念，表現為勤朴古健果義，敢為居安思危，善始善終。

ㄔ眼睛上有一直线，表示一直向前，ㄔ表示道路。心表示心能與眼睛一樣正直。德，意為來去做也不去想那些走小路抄近路的事。

书　　　　　　　BOOK

材质：纸质　　　　Material: paper
规格：71 × 46.5 cm　Height 71 × width 46.5 cm

甲骨文書是手持毛筆在記錄口說話。金文書豐富了書寫的內容，從聿，從者。書的原意是寫字。在中國，寫字從一開始就是一門藝術。甲骨文、金文都是有意識的美感，而非單純記錄符號。周朝貴族要求掌握的六藝"禮樂射御書數"，科舉考試更是沒有好字便沒有機會。

	手持一支笔记录	A hand's holding a writing brush
	重要的话语	Recording of important words
	书写曾经是神圣的事情，是人类文明前进的一大步	Writing used to be sacred to many. It nonetheless symbolizes a milestone progress in human civilization

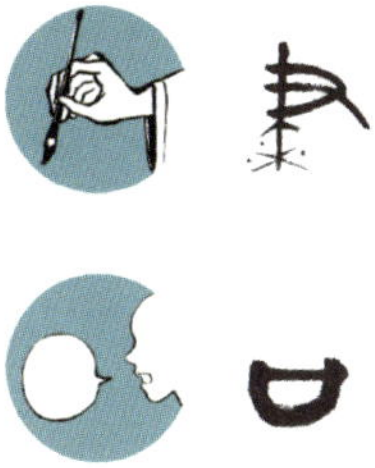

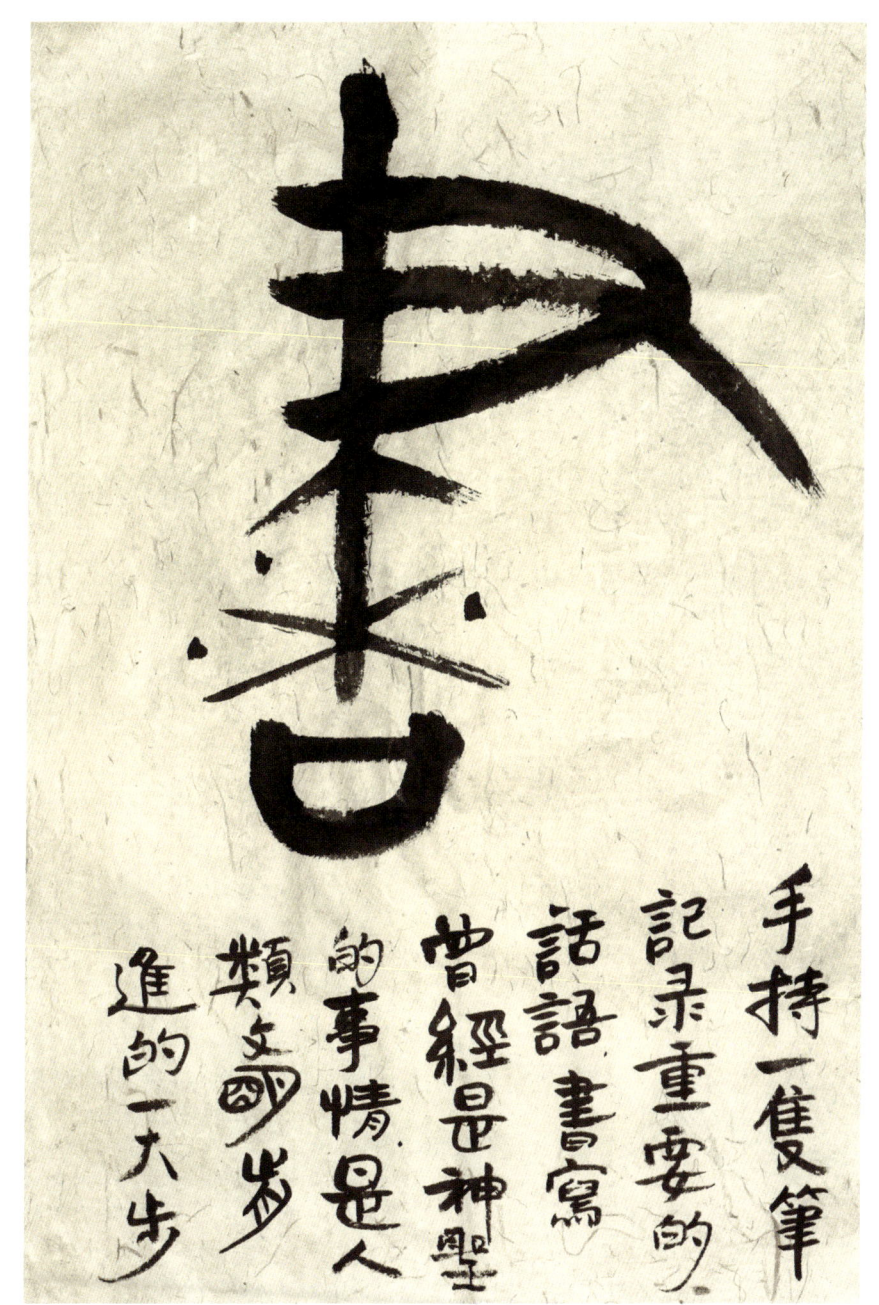

手持一隻筆記錄重要的話語、書寫曾經是神聖的事情,是人類文明的一大步進的一大步

会意字

医　　　　　　　　MEDICAL TREATMENT

材质：纸质　　　　　Material: paper
规格：71 × 46.5 cm　Height 71 × width 46.5 cm

甲骨文医是匚筐匧里攴箭，表示针刺治病针来治病古代很早就有，传说名医扁鹊针刺可起死回生。金文医增加了殳手持器械的意思。小篆醫加酉酒，表示用酒消毒。毉加巫巫，表示古代醫者也是巫师。

酉	酒		Wine
匚	筐匧		A medical cabinet
又	手		A hand
矢	箭矢		An arrow

手持箭矢表示针灸及治疗外伤。酒既可消毒，本身也是药
中医是中国传统文化的重要组成部分，中药、针灸、气功、养生是独到的疗法

An arrow in hand means acupuncture or other surgical treatment. The wine was often used as disinfectant in old days. So it is also a medicine Traditional Chinese Medicine plays an important role in the traditional Chinese culture. Some of its unique treatment includes herbal medicine, acupuncture, Qigong and regimen

酉 匚 殳 矢

醫 手持箭矢表示針灸及治療外傷，酉即西消毒本身也是藥，古人認為上醫醫國，其次疾人，中醫是中國傳統文化重要的組成部分，中藥、針灸、氣功、養生是獨到療法

会意字　097

艺 ART

材质：纸质
规格：71 × 46.5 cm

Material: paper
Height 71 × width 46.5 cm

甲骨文、金文埶均是一人雙手捧土樹苗，表示種植樹木。小篆藝增加了土，隸書藝增加了云，已由種植意轉為浪漫美妙的藝術了。藝字說明，藝術首先是技術，並且恭敬，最後是如雲般變幻莫測。

| | 人跪坐在地上种植树苗 | A man kneels down to plant a sapling |
| | 栽种树苗需要技能，即园艺，引申为艺术。这种恭敬的姿态表明，艺术不仅是手艺，更是一种态度 | Tree planting requires skills, or specifically, gardening skills, which, if extended, can mean craftsmanship. The kneeling posture shows respect, bespeaking an attitude toward art, which therefore cannot be reduced to mere handicraft |

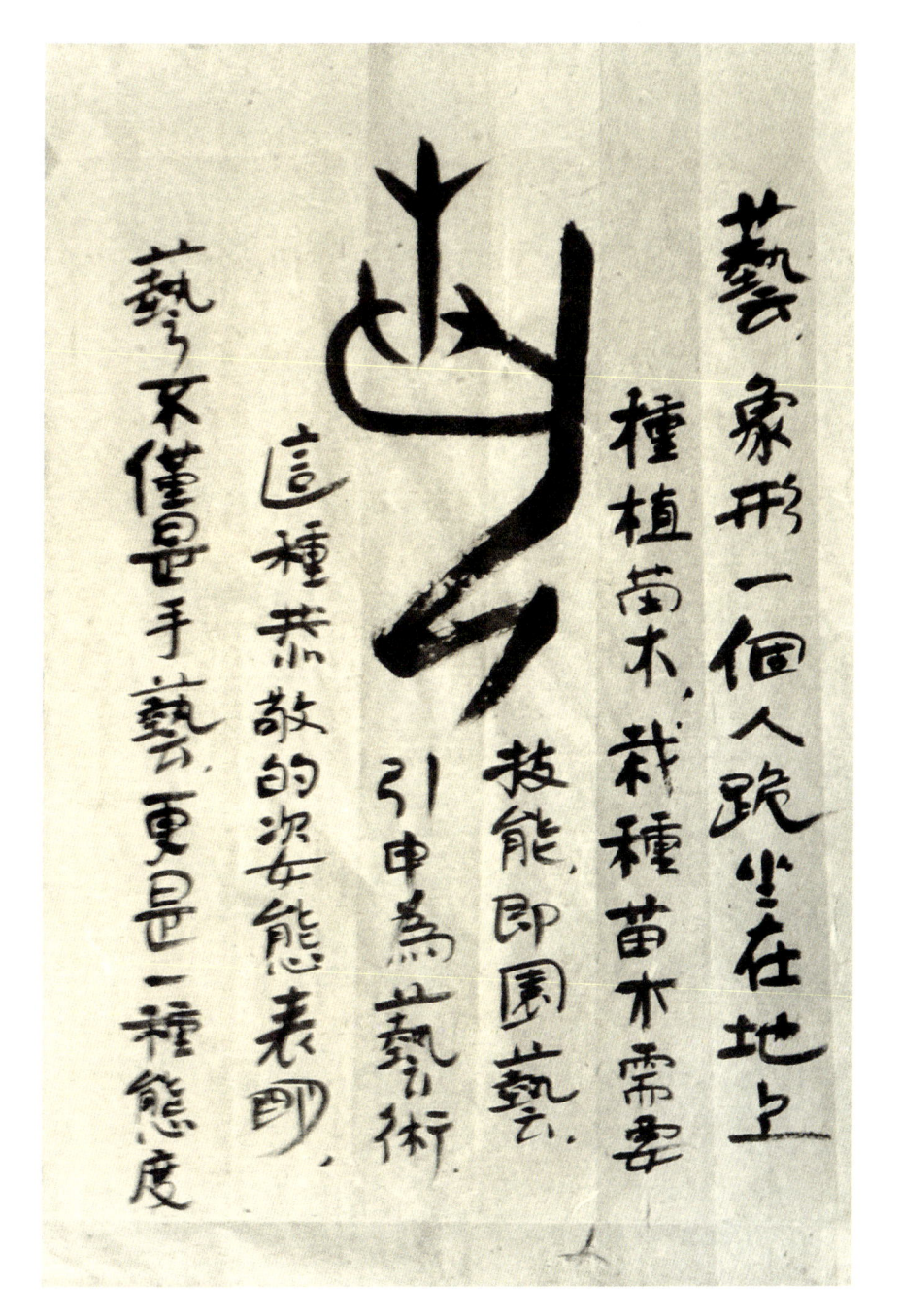

藝，象形，一個人跪坐在地上種植苗木。栽種苗木需要技能，即園藝，引申為藝術。這種恭敬的姿態表明，藝不僅僅是手藝，更是一種態度。

舞　　　　　　　　　DANCE

材质：纸质　　　　　　Material: paper
规格：71 × 46.5 cm　　Height 71 × width 46.5 cm

甲骨文 𣬌 是一人雙手揮舞松枝張口唱歌的象形. 當為祭祀場景. 䙴 增加了雙脚以强調腿部動作. 小篆 舞 再加上雙脚已經有了合於節奏的動感。

古人执松枝按节奏舞蹈、敬神。这是人类艺术的起源。在中国，舞是礼的重要部分

In ancient ages, men performed dance with branches in their hands to show their homage to the God. This is the origin of human art. In the Chinese culture, dancing is regarded as an important component of etiquette

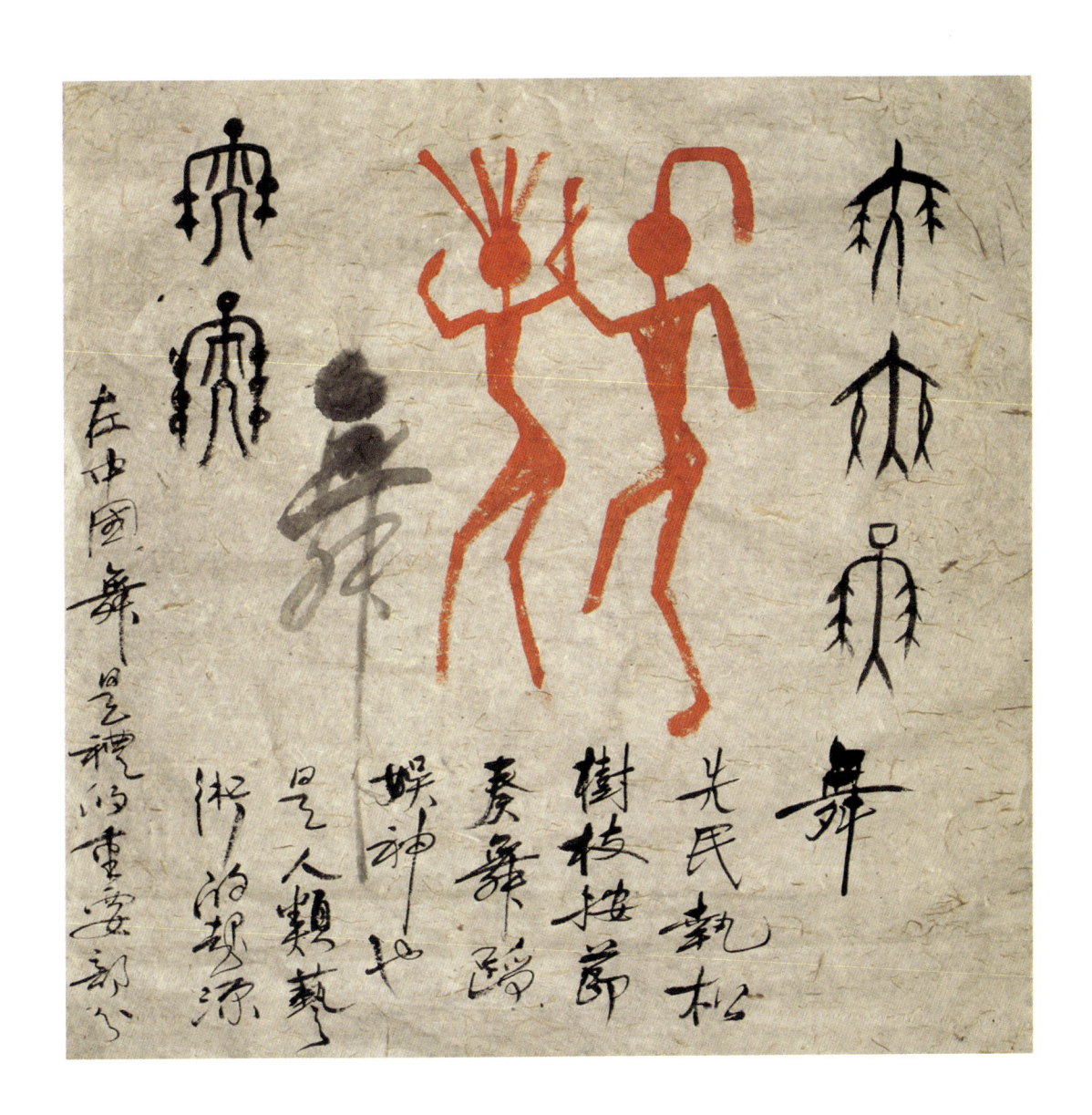

先民執松樹枝按節奏舞蹈娛神也是人類藝術的起源

在中國舞即是禮的重要部分

会意字　101

仁 　　　BENEVOLENCE

材质：纸质 / 竹简 　　Material: paper / bamboo slips
规格：90 × 90 cm 　　Height 90 × width 90 cm

仁是孔子最核心的思想。由个单人旁和二组成。"二"读作"等"，意为齐整、等同。两形组合表示人与人心理上的平等关系。孔子在处理人际关系主张相待以礼，而在心理上则主张在平等原则下的爱人。《说文》说仁、亲也，就是这个意思。

仁

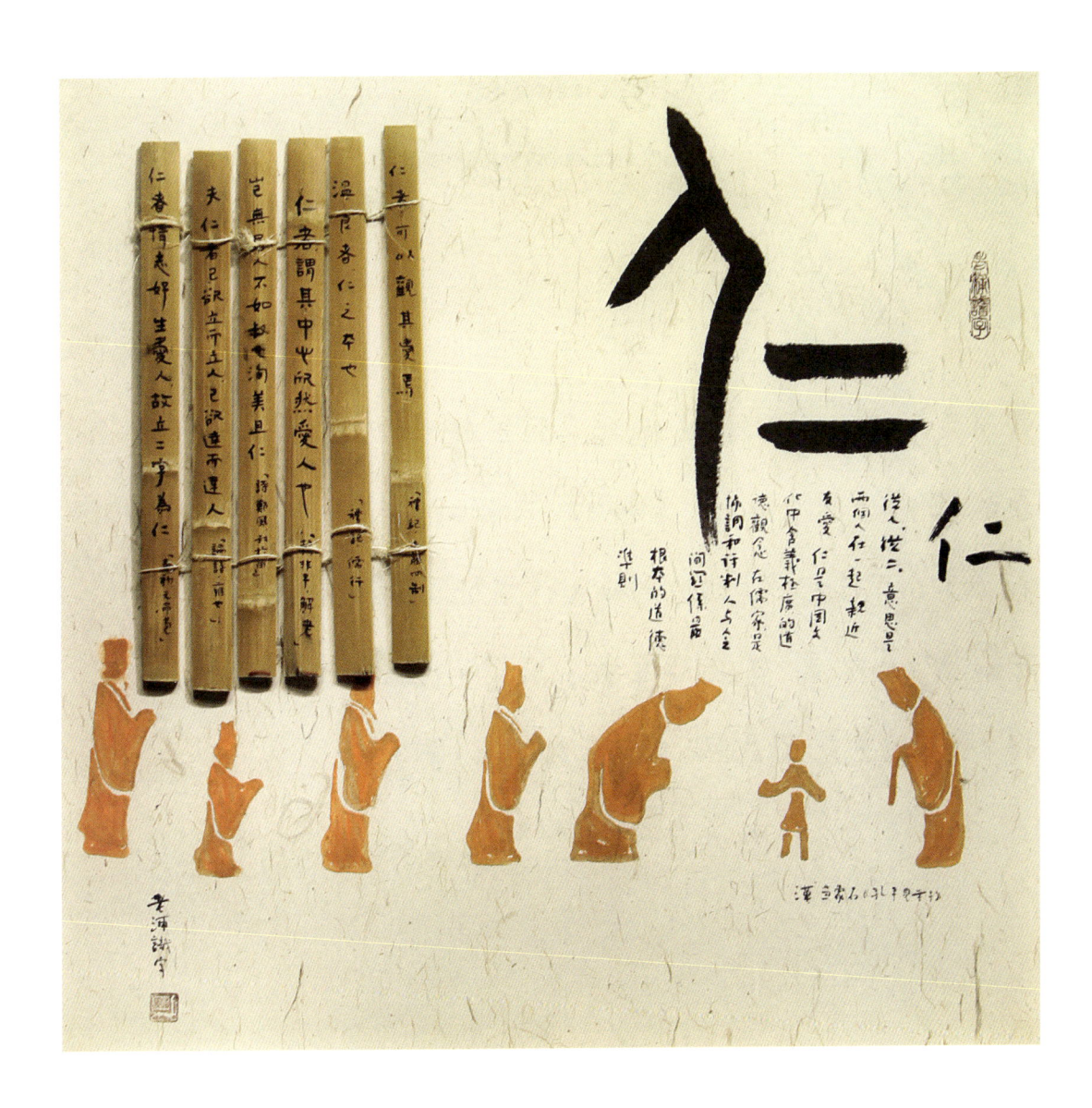

从人从二，意思是两个人在一起很亲爱友爱。仁是中国文化中含义极宽的道德观念，在儒家是体现和谐人际关系的最高准则。

仁者情志好生爱人故立二字为人（正韵新解）

夫仁者己欲立而立人己欲达而达人（论语·雍也）

岂无他人不如我同姓且仁（诗经·郑风·将仲子）

仁者谓其中心欣然爱人也（诗经·郑风·叔于田）

温良者仁之本也（礼记·儒行）

仁者可以观其爱焉（礼记·丧服四制）

老弟识字

会意字　103

义　　　　　RIGHTEOUSNESS

材质：纸质 / 竹简
规格：45.5 × 76 cm

Material: paper / bamboo slips
Height 45.5 × width 76 cm

義字是升我，一種儀仗用的兵器上加一個羊字，表示儀仗上掛著羊頭，羊即祥，吉祥的象徵，兩形相加表示受到神护助佑的吉祥出征。儒家講"忠孝節義"其中"義"是指平輩相交的原則，在士大夫，是捨生取義的道義，在民间，是義氣相投的義氣。

羊義義

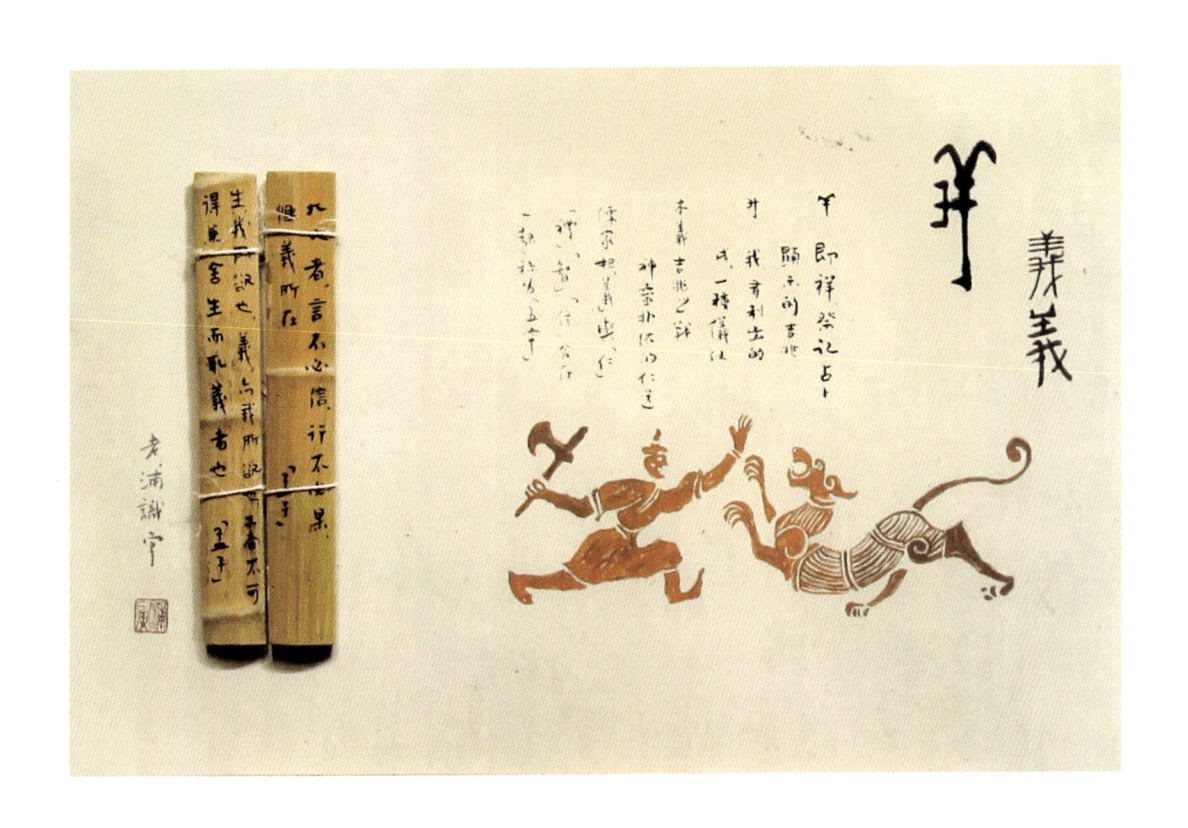

卜即祥祭记占卜
關示向吉地
才我有利出的
戈一样偏让
手義吉也之祥
神奈扑此心行达
保家相其也（他）
吗，吉也食含
一动拼为五千

义（義）者，言不必信，许不必果
即义之所在

九一者言也。义为我所欲，舍生而取义者也。「孟子」

老浦谦宁

会意字　105

礼

CEREMONY

材质：纸质 / 竹简
规格：38 × 38 cm

Material: paper / bamboo slips
Height 38 × width 38 cm

壴是有支架的鼓。玨是成串的玉。凵是盛玉的盘子。合起来意为击鼓敬玉。礼敬上天或与其他部族结交。礼在儒学中成为严格的行为规范。值得注意的是，礼在上古是击鼓大事宣扬的仪式。类似今天的国礼。偷偷摸摸送的不是礼，是贿。

禮

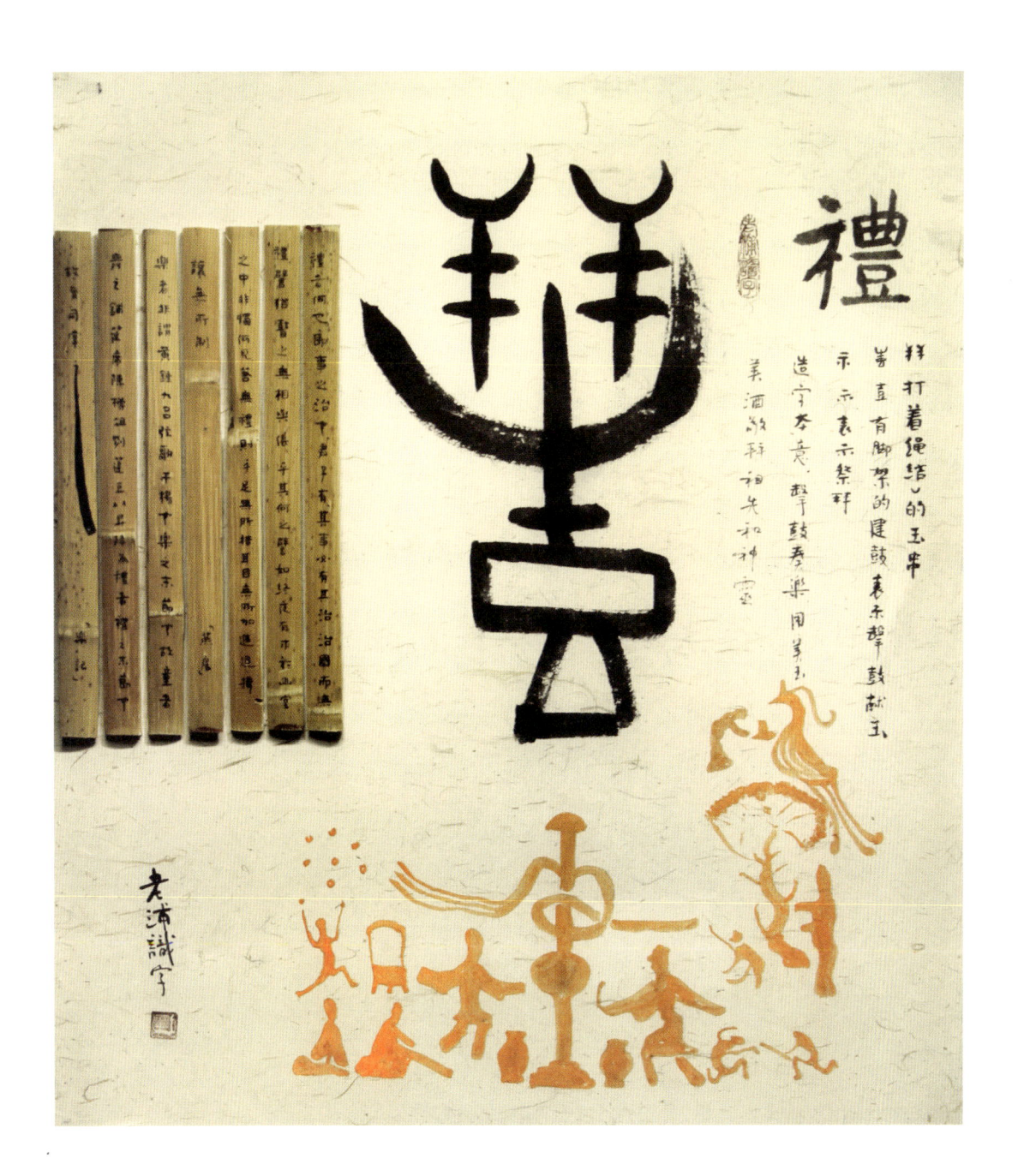

拜，打着繩結 的玉串
箸 真 有腳架的建鼓表示聲鼓獻玉
示 表示祭祀
造字本意：擊鼓奏樂用美玉
美酒敬拜祖先和神靈

老浦識字

会意字 107

智

材质：纸质 / 竹简
规格：100 × 90 cm

WISDOM

Material: paper / bamboo slips
Height 100 × width 90 cm

"个"是箭、矢，"于"是木製武器，"口"是口，"曰"是曰，説的意思。合起来是談論作戰謀略。箭，鋒利並可及遠，象徵思想敏鋭迅捷。口，表示口口相傳，是經驗的積累。曰是論述，表示思想必須經過梳理整合。

智

老浦識字

人箭頭矢代表戰爭
于干木制武器
曰口表示談論
曰說強調表達
造字本意談論作戰謀略

孫子兵法 一則

孫子曰兵者國之大事也
死生之地存亡之道不可不
察也故經之以五校之以計以索
其情一曰道二曰天三曰地四曰將
五曰法道者令民與上同意者
也故可與之死可與之生民弗詭
也天者陰陽寒暑時制也順逆
兵勝也地者高下廣狭遠近險易
生也將者智信仁勇嚴也法者曲
制官道主用也凡此五者將莫
不聞知之者勝不知者不勝故校之以
計而索其情曰主孰有道將孰有
能天地孰得法令孰行兵眾孰
強士卒孰練賞罰孰明吾以此知
勝負矣

信

BELIEVE / BELIEVE IN / TRUST

材质：纸质
规格：69.5 × 46.5 cm

Material: paper
Height 69.5 × width 46.5 cm

金文化是单人旁加一個口，表示開口承諾。有的金文信是"千"加"言"言，表示千言萬語地保證。《說文》信，誠也。在上古，沒有契约，説話算數，一諾千金。民間有："一個吐沫一個釘"的説法。現在契约社會，口説無凭。

信

只人的结合即为信，意为言而有信才为信。人在中国古代人们用说话算数代替契约，而对於士则是君无戏言而对於君王则言必有信。一言九鼎，二言九鼎，言必有信

吞浦识字

会意字　111

真　　REAL / GENUINE / AUTHENTIC

材质：纸质 / 树皮　　Material: paper / bark
规格：35 × 45.8 cm　　Height 35 × width 45.8 cm

甲骨文真由卜(卜)占卜和鼎鼎组成。意为用鼎占卜的人。与贞同源。《說文》真，仙人變形而登天也。《庄子·渔父》真者，精誠之至也...真在內者，神動於外，是所以貴真也。

眞

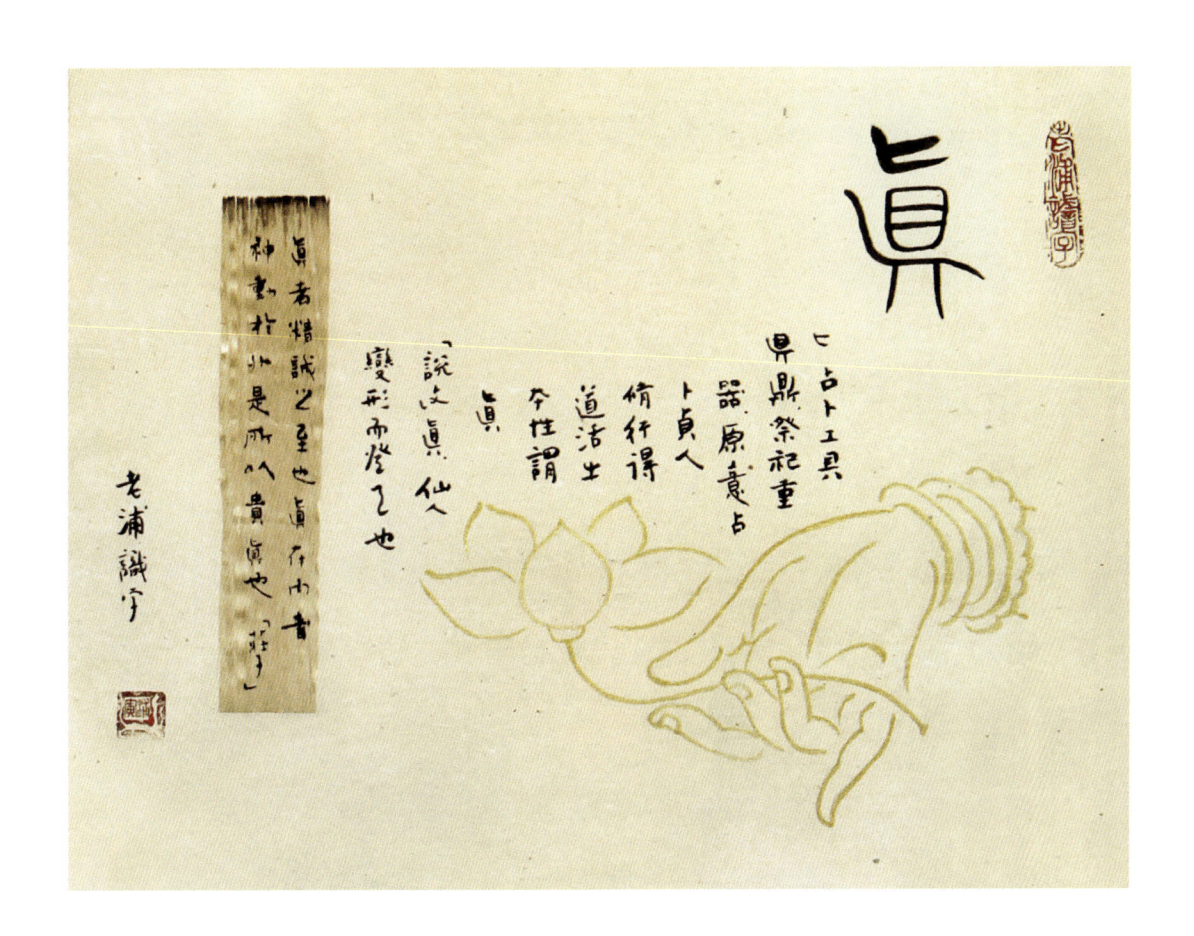

卜占卜工具
鼎鼎祭祀重
器。原意占
卜貞人
修行得
道活生
今性謂
眞
"說文真,仙人
變形而登之也

真者精誠之至也,真在不真
神動於外是所以貴真也。"莊子"

老浦識字

众	MULTITUDE
材质：纸质 规格：69.5 × 46.5 cm	Material: paper Height 69.5 × width 46.5 cm

甲骨文眾，日表示目標，三個人表示人數多，兩形會意表示很多人往一個目標前進。金文眾上面变成了眼睛，表示很多人方向一致。隶書眾上面的目变成血，是歃血为盟吗？楷書眾有雄渾的美感，简化字众一人统领，威风，只是失去了目標。

会意字 115

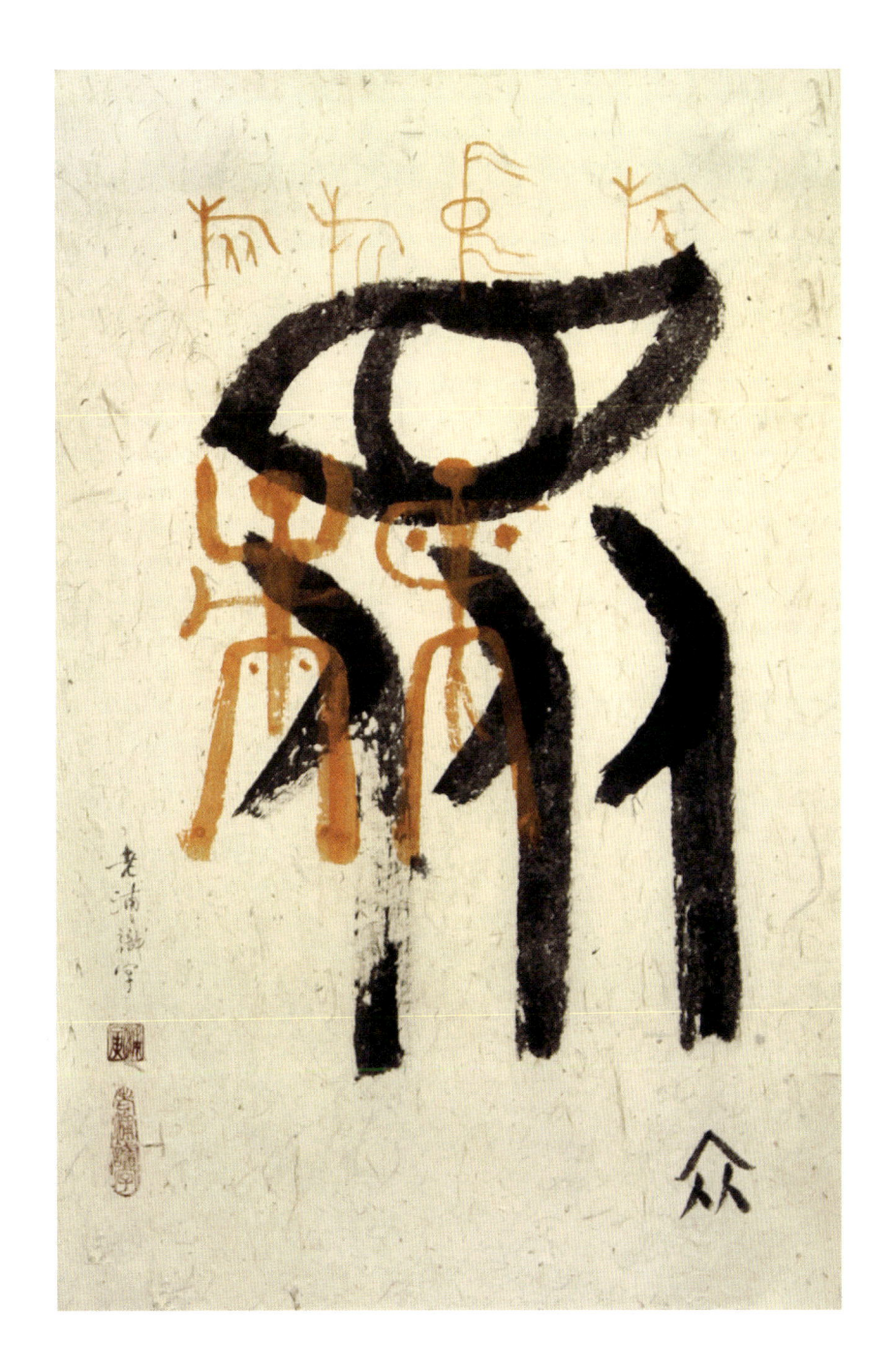

买　　　　　　　　BUY

材质：纸质　　　　Material: paper
规格：69.5 × 46.5 cm　　Height 69.5 × width 46.5 cm

甲骨文買，从网，旳貝是古代货币，两形会意表示网盛货币去市场購物。今人購物，也是上网，真乃天意。購物之欲，与如天网，别手奈何。商品交易，与如天网，纵横无往不致。

買

网，古人交易的容器
的貝，古錢幣
凡貝字旁皆与货币有关

古人买卖交易用网作容器
今人用网购物奉事越来
意乎。只是古人也告诉我们
买东西的欲望就是一张网
剁手都没用

浦寅

会意字　117

坐

SIT

材质：纸质
规格：69.5 × 46.5 cm

Material: paper
Height 69.5 × width 46.5 cm

甲骨文 㘴 反映了古人的坐姿，下面是席子。金文 坐 将席子改为土，又增一人形，当是农耕人们席地而坐的反映。小篆 坐 将二人改为两留，以表示止息之意。隶书坐改四二人。在汉魏有胡床之前，古人均跪坐。

坐

卩，跪姿
囗，席子
古人的坐姿
是跪踞，
所以跪才说
坐，席不正不坐

会意字

走　　　　　　　　　RUN

材质：纸质　　　　　　Material: paper
规格：69.5× 46.5 cm　　Height 69.5 × width 46.5 cm

走，在古代表示跑。大夭，是行走的姿态。止止是脚印的象形，表示行进。在古代，走是甘步，跑是奋走，快跑是蠢奔。

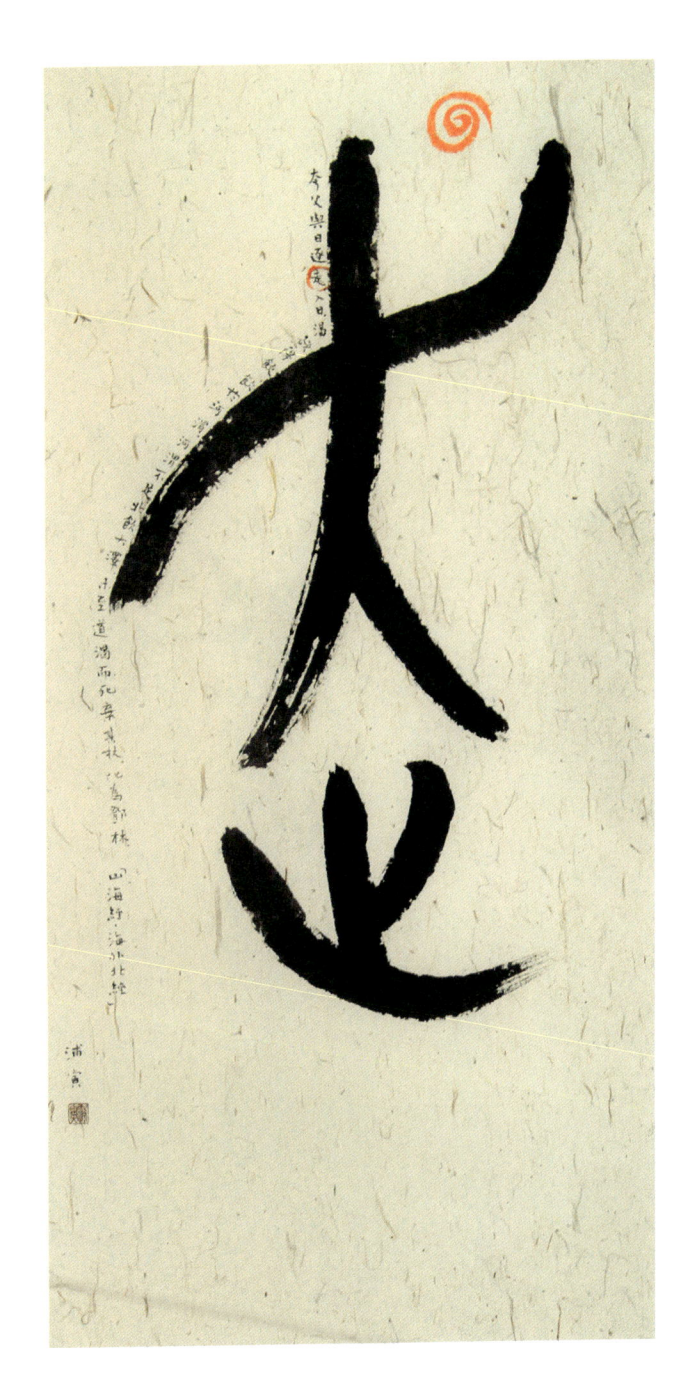

会意字

涉　　　　WADE

材质：纸质
规格：46.5 × 69.5 cm

Material: paper
Height 46.5 × width 69.5 cm

涉．一條河流～，兩個腳印 ，這是"步"，兩個腳印一个在河這邊．一個在河對岸．表于涉水過河．既然下了水．河．一定要過去。

楚人有涉江者其劍自舟中墜於水遽契其舟曰
是吾劍之所從墜江舟止從其所契者入水求之舟已行矣
而劍不行求劍若此不亦惑乎
「呂氏春秋·察今」

浦紫

会意字 123

刑

CORPORAL PUNISHMENT / PHYSICAL TORTURE

材质：纸质
规格：69.5 × 46.5 cm

Material: paper
Height 69.5 × width 46.5 cm

金文丼ㄌ，丼乃套在头上的木枷，ㄌ是刀。《说文》荆。型也意为割颈砍头。上古五刑是墨劓、宫、刖、大辟即刺字、割鼻、割生殖器、斩足、死刑。中古五刑自魏晋南北朝分别是死、流、耐、鞭、杖。封建制五刑笞、杖、徒、流、死。

刑

浦寅

会意字　125

死

DIE / DEATH

材质：纸质
规格：69.5 × 46.5 cm

Material: paper
Height 69.5 × width 46.5 cm

死生亦大矣。这是古人对死亡的感慨。死亡也是古今文艺作品永恒的题材。汉字死，一个跪坐的人形，旁边一具骨植。那悲伤的感情从他低垂的头、低偻的身形就能感受出来。

会意字 127

善

GOODNESS

材质：纸质
规格：70×70 cm

Material: paper
Height 70 × width 70 cm

甲骨文𦎫、䚩、𦏃都是夸张了羊的大眼睛，还有显得温顺的弯角。金文增加了两个言，表示言语祥合。简化的善基本保留了原意。羊是古人生活、祭祀的重要动物，羊旁多有吉祥之意。

善良的心就是太阳
——雨果

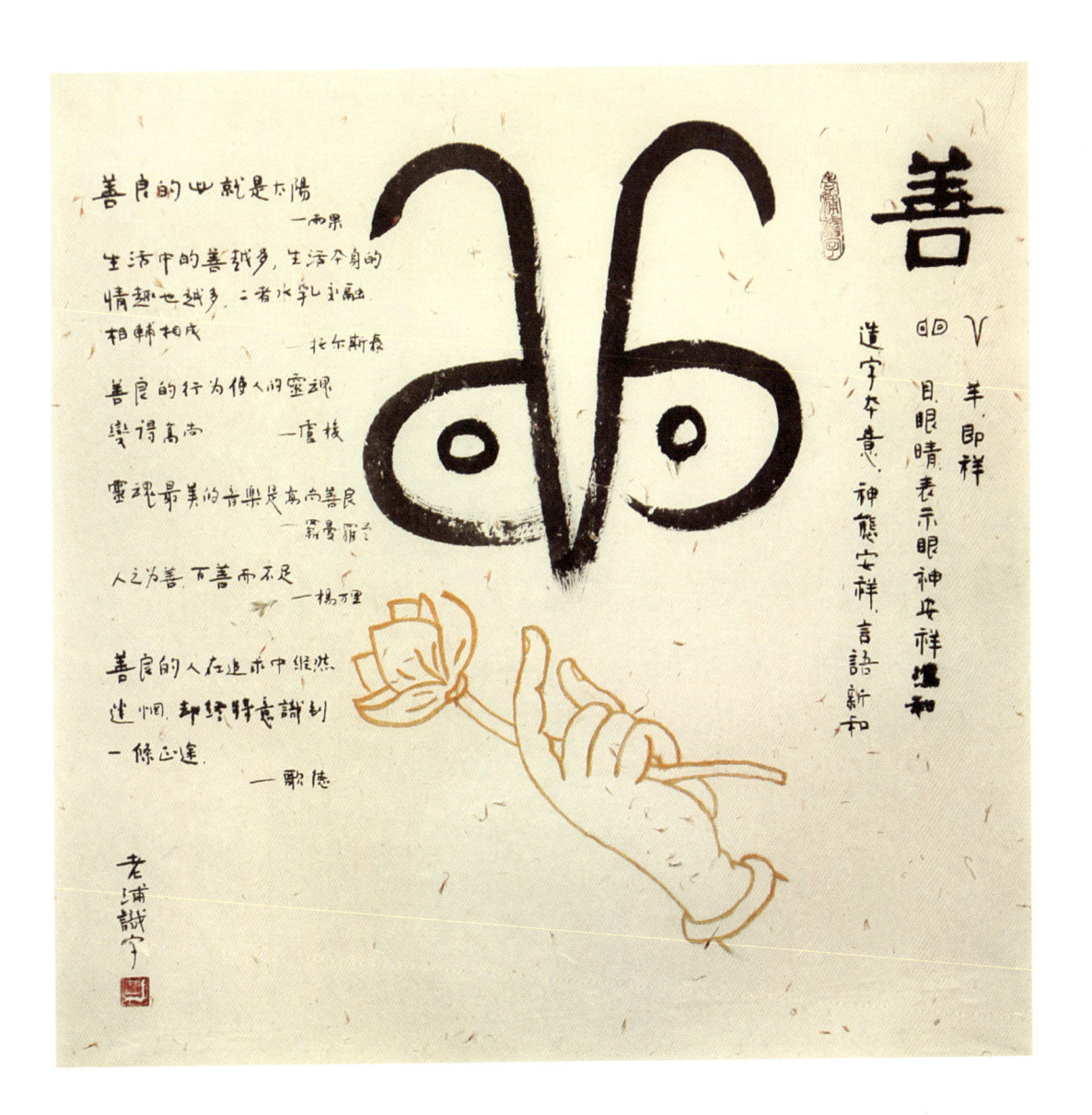

生活中的善越多，生活个身的
情趣也越多，二者水乳交融，
相辅相成。
——托尔斯泰

善良的行为使人的灵魂
变得高尚。——卢梭

灵魂最美的音乐是高尚善良
——罗曼罗兰

人之为善，百善而不足
——杨万里

善良的人在追求中纵然
迷惘，却终将意识到
一条正途。——歌德

老浦识字

善

羊 即 祥
目 眼睛 表示眼神安祥温和

造字本意 神态安祥 言语新和

会意字　129

保   PROTECT / PROTECTION

材质：纸质 / 特种手工纸   Material: paper / handmade paper
规格：36× 31 cm   Height 36× width 31 cm

甲骨文 保 是一人反抱一子，表示保护孩子。金文 保 延袭了甲骨文字型。缘于古人外出，须将孩子背在背上方保安全。金文 保 改为正面抱子保护，意义更加清晰。篆文保已经看不出原意了。

保

「說文」保，養也
保護兒童乃人類
本能乃全社會之
責任

老浦識字

会意字　131

尿　　　　　　　　　URINE

材质：纸质　　　　　　Material: paper
规格：69.5× 46.5 cm　　Height 69.5× width 46.5 cm

甲骨文为在人个的下腹部飞三点，表示男人小便，非常形象。图中的《金刚经》是一点个人的体悟。佛法在生活中，在日常中，随顺一切却不堕一切。无所谓污秽，心清净，处处皆净土。

如是我聞一時佛在
舍衛國祇樹給孤獨
園與大比丘眾千二百
人俱爾時世尊食時
著衣持鉢入舍衛城

会意字

屎   EXCREMENT / FECES

材质：纸质
规格：69.5×46.5 cm

Material: paper
Height 69.5× width 46.5 cm

甲骨文𡱁，在人勹的下部加点指事符号，表示排泄物。篆文屎在尸尾下加米表示排泄物，现代汉字屎表示秽物的尸骨体，也很传神。周中佛经与污泥中的莲花同理，于污秽处行清净法。

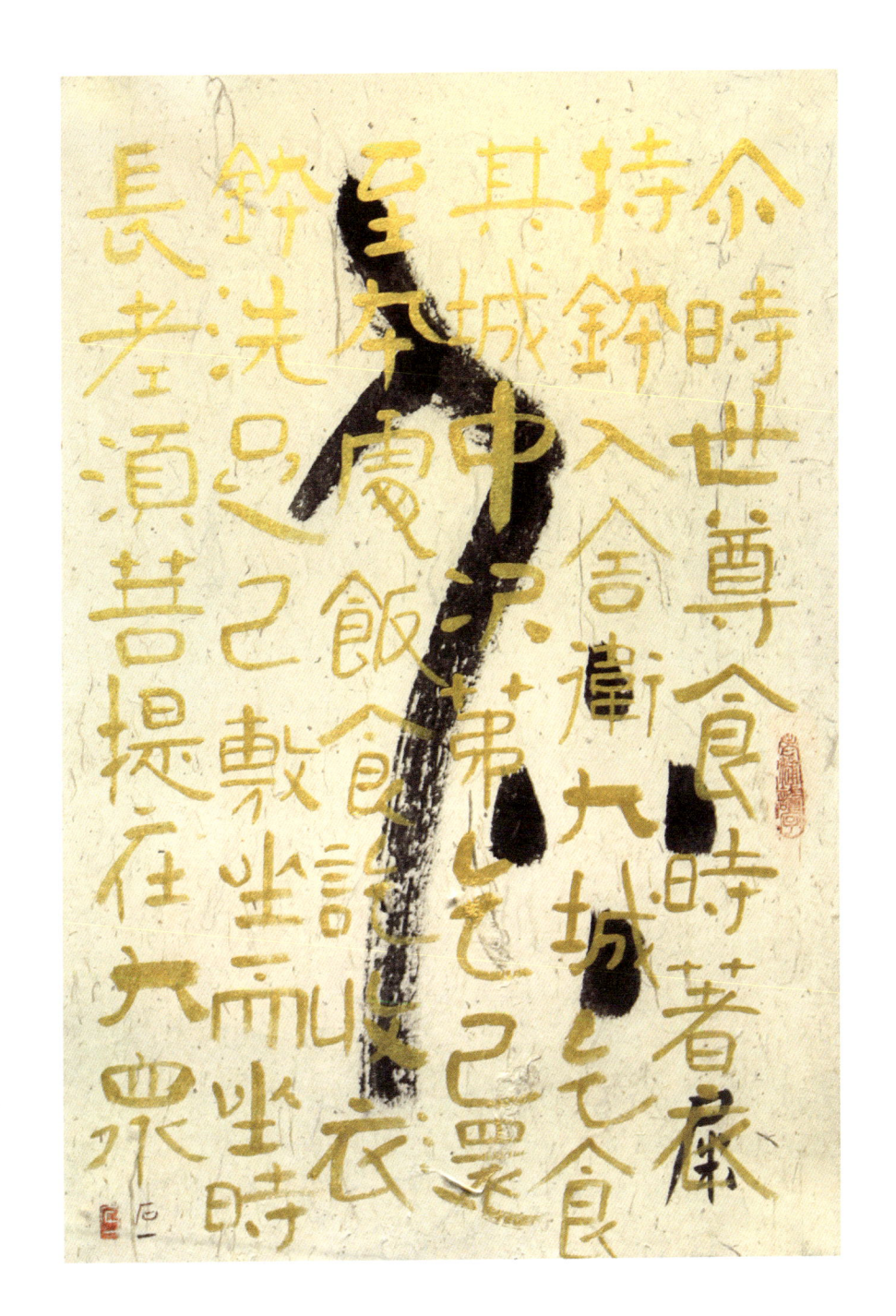

会意字

益　　　　　　　　BENEFIT

材质：纸质　　　　　Material: paper
规格：69.5 × 46.5 cm　Height 69.5 × width 46.5 cm

甲骨文🖼，乙是皿，盛水的容器，∵是水，从皿口溢出。金文益，八的造字意更明确。小篆益将水改为横向，沿革至今。《说文》益，富饶有盈余，所以引伸为好。原意另造溢字。

半半歌

看破浮生過半，半之受用無邊。半中歲月盡悠閒，半裡乾坤開展。
半郭半鄉村舍，半山半水田園。半耕半讀半經塵，半士半民姻眷。
半雅半粗器具，半華半實庭軒。衾裳半素半輕鮮，肴饌半豐半儉。
童僕半能半拙，妻兒半樸半賢。心情半佛半神仙，姓字半藏半顯。
一半還之天地，讓得一半人間。半思後代與滄田，半想閻羅怎見。
酒飲半酣正好，花開半時偏妍。帆張半扇免翻顛，馬放半韁穩便。
半少卻饒滋味，半多反厭糾纏。百年苦樂半相參，會占便宜只半。

李密庵　　溥儒

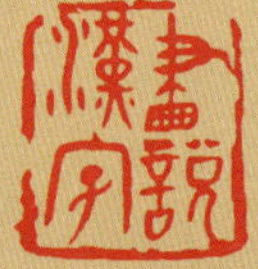
畫說漢字

主题字组

COMPOSITE
WORDS

关于男人的字　　WORDS ABOUT MEN

材质：纸质　　　　　　Material: paper
规格：69.5×46.5 cm　　Height 69.5× width 46.5 cm

	母腹中的胎儿	A fetus in the womb
	儿童	A child
	儿童已经长大	The child has grown up
	18 岁的成年男子	An 18-year-old adult man
	胸口刺满纹身的勇武男人	A brave man with tattoos all over his breast
	两个男人并排去狩猎或打仗	Two men hunting or fighting side by side
	背负重物的人，表现一生的体力劳动	A man carrying a heavy load on his back, meaning lifelong manual labor
	男人腋下中箭，表现在劳动或打仗中受伤	An armpit pricked with an arrow, meaning a man wounded at work or on the battleground
	拄拐杖的老人，表现劳碌一生的男人的暮年	An old man leaning on a cane, meaning the aging years of a hard-labored man
	跪坐在尸体边的人，表现死亡	A mournful man kneeling down beside a corpse, meaning the demise of a man

巳 Embryos

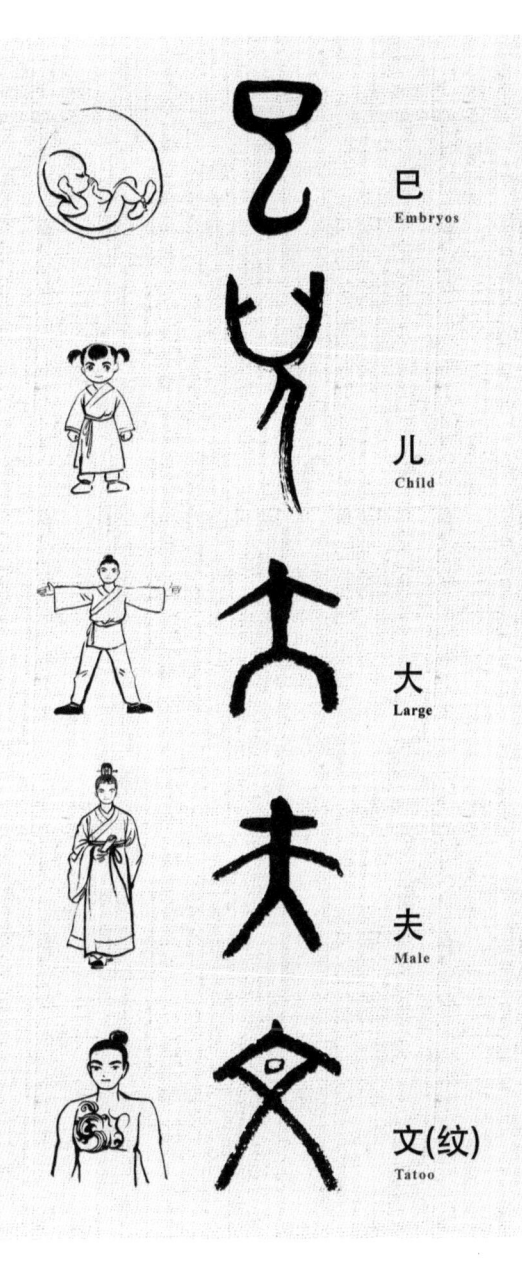

儿 Child

大 Large

夫 Male

文(纹) Tatoo

并 Together with

重 Load

疾 Injury

老 Old

死 Die

主题字组

关于女人的字　　WORDS ABOUT WOMEN

材质：纸质　　Material: paper
规格：69.5 × 46.5 cm　　Height 69.5 × width 46.5 cm

	跪坐着的女人	A kneeling woman
	女人头顶上有只手，表示她在男人面前安定了	A hand shown above a woman's head, meaning she is subdued by a man
	"若（诺）"，少女散开头发承诺与心仪的男人一起生活	A lass loosens her hair to show her determination to live together with the man she loves
	一只手抓住女人，表现原始社会抢亲的风俗	A man's hand grabbing a woman's, representing the ancient custom of bride snatching
	女人怀孕，肚子里有个孩子	A pregnant woman, with a fetus seen in her body
	中部加两个点，用哺乳女人的大乳房表现母亲	The two dots in the middle depict the large breasts of a nursing mother
	母亲哺乳，孩子在母亲的怀抱里张大了小嘴	The mother is breast feeding her baby, who opens its small mouth widely while lying in her mother's arms
	女人和孩子，在中国古代，女人能带好孩子是最好的事	A woman and a child, in ancient China, it is the best if a woman can take good care of her baby
	女人和小树苗，表示氏族的繁衍全靠女性	A woman and a sapling, meaning the whole clan relies on the women to extend the lineage

女 Female

妥 Appropriate

若 Promise

妻 Wife

孕 Pregnant

母 Mother

乳 Breast-feed

好 Good

姓 Family name

主题字组

天气

WEATHER

材质：纸质
规格：69.5 × 46.5 cm

Material: paper
Height 69.5 × width 46.5 cm

風 一個是鳳鳥邊一個表示空洞的符號H、表示空中使鳳鳥飛翔的气流。 气．氣流的象形

云．云和雲是二意．云本意为说雲指天上的雲朵．由水氣構成　雨：天上揮下的水滴．雪 霖．羽．雨．水羽毛狀飄落物　雷．雷．雨．飞閃電．石頭般砸来的轟鳴聲．伴著雨．閃電的巨响．

风 Wind	气 Qi	云 Cloud
雨 Rain	雪 Snow	雷 Thunder

动物　　　　　　　ANIMALS

材质：纸质　　　　　Material: paper
规格：69.5×46.5 cm　Height 69.5× width 46.5 cm

这是一组传神的象形字，简捷准确地抓住了动物最突出的特征。象强调了庞大的身躯和长鼻，豹强调斑纹，龟是俯视图，蜂是细腿，虫是蛇头，狐回头张望表现诡情，鹿是角和轻盈的身体。

象 Elephant

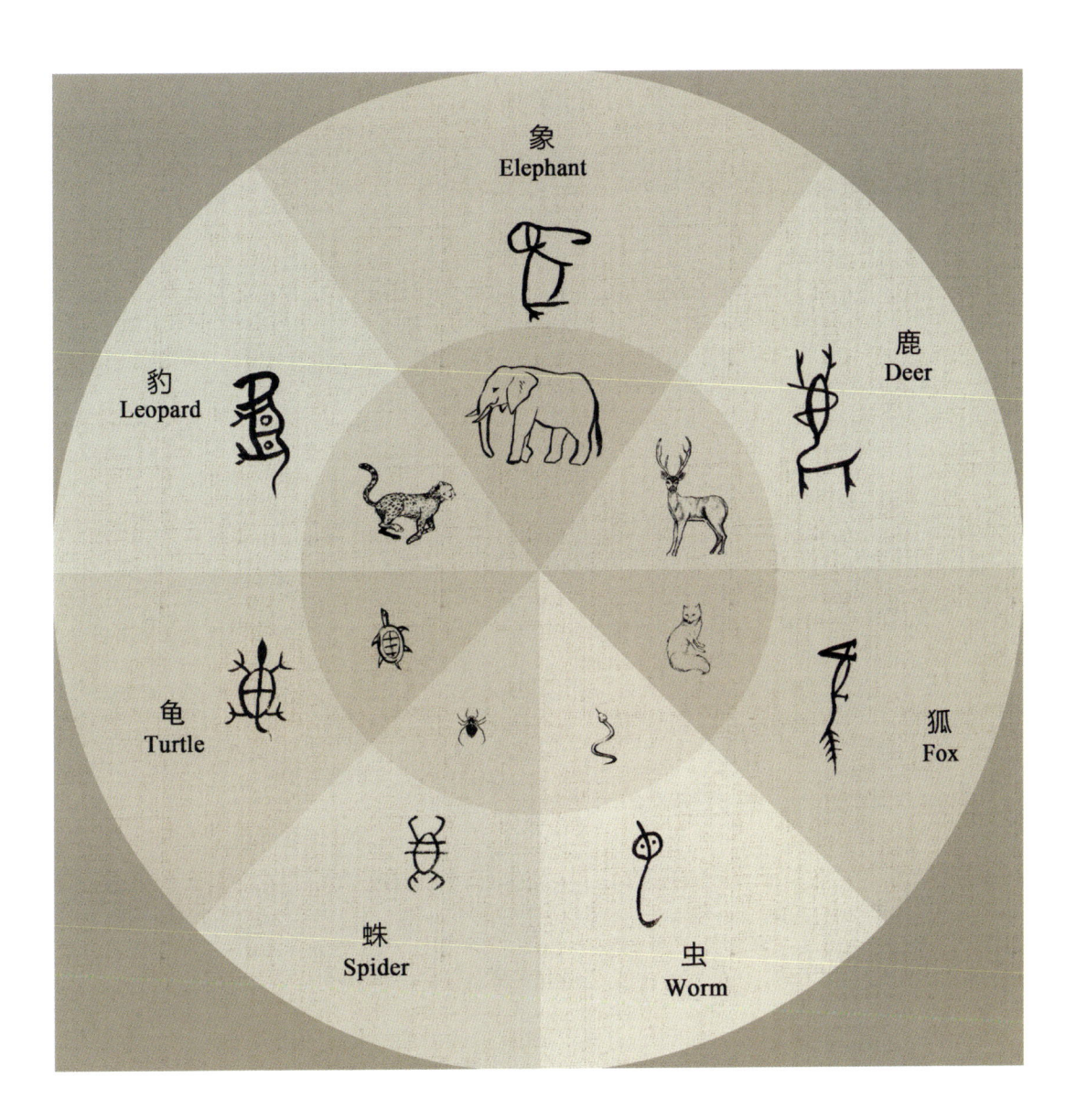

鹿 Deer

豹 Leopard

狐 Fox

龟 Turtle

蛛 Spider

虫 Worm

主题字组

城垣	CITY WALL
材质：老粗布 规格：69.5 × 46.5 cm	Material: paper Height 69.5 × width 46.5 cm

		播种的小坑	A hole dug in the ground for seed sowing
		手的象形	The image of a hand
		铲土的工具	An ancient implement for shoveling earth
		土的象形	The symbol for earth
		衣服的象形。合起来的意思是脱掉衣服帮助播种。本意为帮助	The symbol for clothes. When combined, these symbols mean the action of taking off the coat to help sow seeds. They originally mean assistance
		城墙延绵不断的象形	The symbol for endless stretching of city walls
		土的象形。合起来的意思是用土夯实的城墙	The symbol for earth. They are combined to mean the rammed earth structure of city walls

城垣的形成是文明发展的重要阶段。2500年前，晋国贵族赵襄子在今天的山西修筑长城。为纪念此事，此地被称为"襄垣"，这个地名延续使用了两千多年都没有变过，是中国最古老的地名之一	The formation of city walls is a milestone in the history of Chinese civilization. Back in 2,500 B.C., Zhao Xiangzi (with the middle word of "xiang" as the phonetic expression of "assistance"), an aristocrat from a vassal state "Jin" had earth walls built around the state, where Shanxi Province is located today. The very location of these walls was then named "Xiangyuan" (the combined phonetic versions of "assistance" and "wall") by locals for them to commemorate this event. Ever since then, "Xiangyuan" has remained unchanged for over 2,000 years, deserving to be one of the oldest place name in China

襄 Assistance　　　　垣 Wall

主题字组

叠加字

COMPOUND
IDEOGRAPHS
(IDENTIEAL COMPONENTS)

人、从、众　　PERSON, ONEFOLLOWING ANOTHER, MULTITUDE

材质：纸质
规格：69.5 × 46.5 cm

Material: paper
Height 69.5 × width 46.5 cm

人、从、众

人：入，一個躬身勞作的人形

從：从，兩人一前一後相隨而行。从是甲骨另一個寫法，從 金文加上（脚），繁骨野字從

众：三人通常指眾多。

𠂉	人	Man
从	从	One following another
众	众	Multitude

叠加字 153

木、林、森　　TREE, WOODS, FOREST

材质：纸质　　　　　　　Material: paper
规格：69.5×46.5 cm　　　Height 69.5 × width 46.5 cm

木：🌱 樹的象形，重要的偏旁。

林：二木为林。

森：三木为森，甲骨文也有森的写法。

木	木	Tree
林	林	Woods
森	森	Forest

叠加字

叠加字 155

火、炎、焱　　　　FIRE, FLAMES, BLAZE

材质：纸质
规格：69.5×46.5 cm

Material: paper
Height 69.5 × width 46.5 cm

火：甲骨文 ⛢ 乃火苗的象形，篆文火与今同。

炎：二火相叠表示火焰延绵，最早用火的首领被称为炎帝

焱（yàn），光焰，《说文》焱，光华也。

	火	Fire
	炎	Flames
	焱	Blaze

叠加字 157

石、砳、磊

材质：纸质
规格：69.5×46.5 cm

STONE, AN ONOMATOPOEIA MEANING "THE SOUND OF STONES COLLIDING WITH EACH OTHER", PILING UP OF STONES

Material: paper
Height 69.5 × width 46.5 cm

石：阝口，阝是悬崖，口是岩块。

砳（lè），石头撞击声

磊（lěi），多石，也指胸襟开阔

石	石	Stone
砳	砳	An Onomatopoeia meansing "the sound of stones colliding with each other"
磊	磊	Piling up of stones

石 砳 磊

叠加字 159

鹿、麤、塵 DEER, GOING AFAR, DUST

材质：纸质
规格：69.5×46.5 cm

Material: paper
Height 69.5 × width 46.5 cm

鹿．鹿的象形．夸张了它美丽的角。

麤（chū）塵．鹿群扬起的土。

塵（cū）同粗

🦌	鹿	Deer
🦌	麤	Going afar
🦌	塵	Dust

160　叠加字

叠加字 161

鱼、鱻、渔

材质：纸质
规格：69.5×46.5 cm

FISH, THE TRADITIONAL CHINESE CHARACTER FOR "FRESH OR DELICIOUS", FISHING

Material: paper
Height 69.5× width 46.5 cm

鱼：鱼的象形。

鱻（xiān），古同鲜。

渔：捕鱼。

	鱼	Fish
	鱻	The taraditional chinese character for "fresh or delicious"
	渔	Fishing

叠加字 163

手 HAND

材质：纸质
规格：69.5×46.5 cm

Material: paper
Height 69.5 × width 46.5 cm

这是一组关于手的汉字。手是甲骨文右手的意思。由这个元件组成有趣的汉字，非常生动地反映了早期人类生活的情景。右手拿一根棍，是"尹"，官吏的意思。右手拿笔，是"津"，负责书写的书吏。手放在门上，是"启"，表示开门。手拿一串丝线，是"系"，表示把东西系在一起。手里斜拿着一根棍，边上一只羊，是"牧"，放牧的意思。

聿
Instruct
负责书写的官吏。
Holding a brush, symbolizes Officers who are responsible for documentation.

尹
Rule
手持木棍，表示官吏。
Holding a stick, symbolizes

毛笔
Writing brush

木棍
Wooden club

启
Open
手放在门上，表示开门。
Opening a door

门
Door

又（右手）
Right hand

系
Tie
手拿丝线，表示把东西系在一起。
Holding silk thread stands for tying something.

丝
Silk

羊
Sheep

牧
Grazing
手拿棍牧羊，意为放牧。
Holding a stick and sheepherding stand for pasturing.

叠加字　165

双手 BOTH HANDS

材质：纸质
规格：69.5 × 46.5 cm

Material: paper
Height 69.5 × width 46.5 cm

雙手丷丷捧起有恭敬、真誠的意思。共是供的原字。具、弄都与祭祀有关。雙手持戈也有士兵整肃之意。雙手相交是朋友。雙手解救是抍的原字，均有真誠之意。

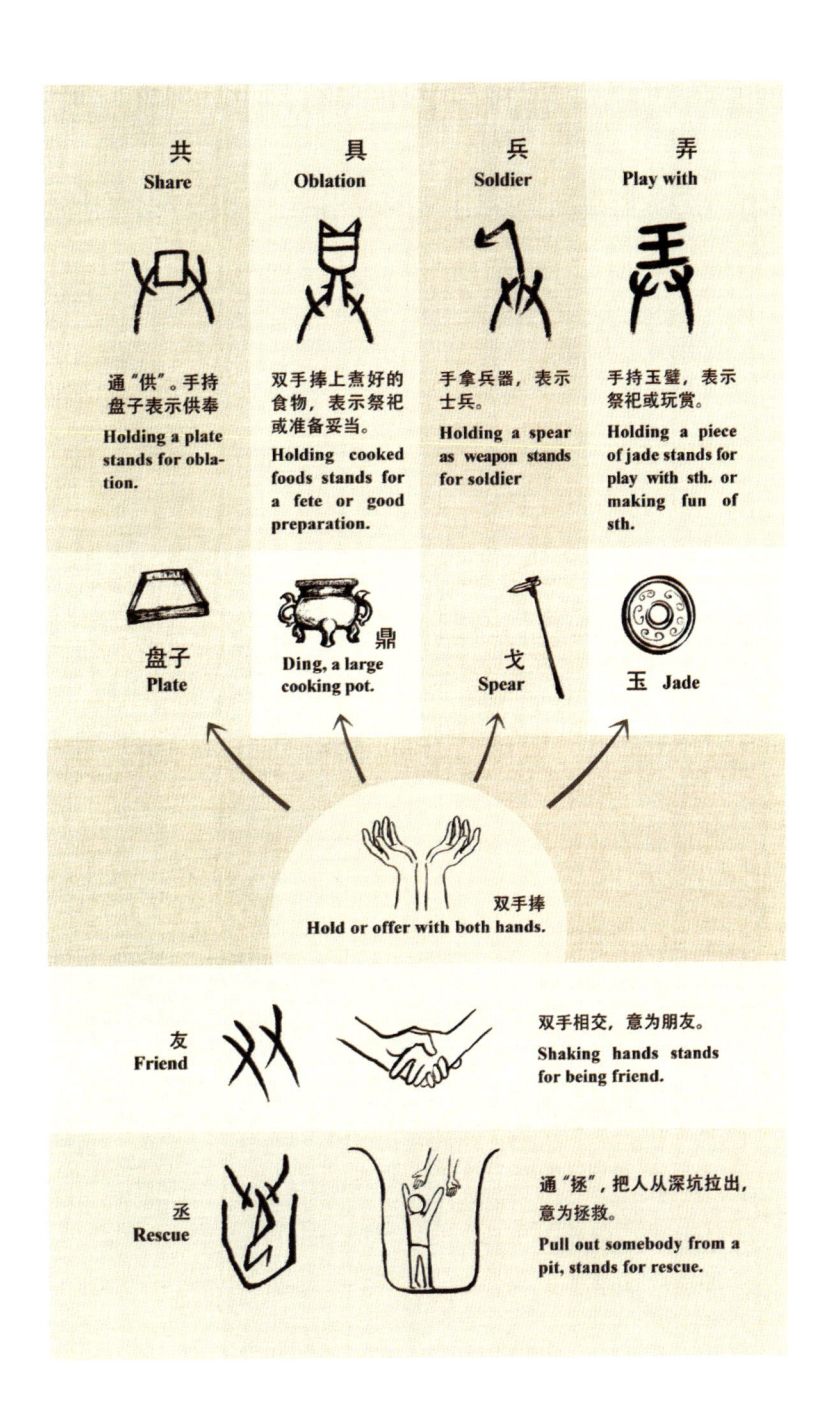

共 Share	具 Oblation	兵 Soldier	弄 Play with
通"供"。手持盘子表示供奉 Holding a plate stands for oblation.	双手捧上煮好的食物，表示祭祀或准备妥当。Holding cooked foods stands for a fete or good preparation.	手拿兵器，表示士兵。Holding a spear as weapon stands for soldier	手持玉璧，表示祭祀或玩赏。Holding a piece of jade stands for play with sth. or making fun of sth.
盘子 Plate	鼎 Ding, a large cooking pot.	戈 Spear	玉 Jade

双手捧 Hold or offer with both hands.

友 Friend		双手相交，意为朋友。Shaking hands stands for being friend.

丞 Rescue		通"拯"，把人从深坑拉出，意为拯救。Pull out somebody from a pit, stands for rescue.

目　　　　　　　　　　EYE

材质：纸质　　　　　　Material: paper
规格：69.5×46.5 cm　　Height 69.5× width 46.5 cm

目，是眼睛的形象。把"目"放在不同的環境中，就組成不同的文字。目字上面加上一条直线中，就是"直"，表示直视前方。目字下面加上一个人體罒，就是"見"，表示看见。這個大眼睛的人坐在一个水盆邊上罒，就是"鉴"，表示用盆里的水照镜子。更仔細的觀察是在太阳下面的很多絲线罒，絲线很細，必须在光亮的地方才能看清，這是"显"。而把"目"放在悬崖下面罒，在如此局促的地方，眼光當然会有局限，就是"限"了。要是站在一個土堆上，那當然是登高望遠的"望"了。

直
Straight

限
Limit

见
See

鉴
Look into the mirror

显
Look carefully

望
Lookout

叠加字　169

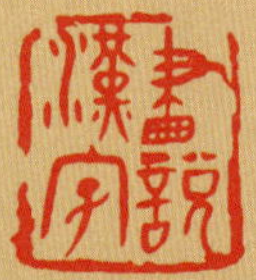
畫說漢字

十二生肖

TWELVE ZODIAC
SIGNS

鼠   RAT / MOUSE

材质：宋锦   Material: Song brocade
规格：69.5×46.5 cm   Height 69.5× width 46.5 cm

甲骨文的"鼠"突出了鼠类的利齿和长尾。上面三点是木屑。鼠是啮齿动物，门齿终生都在生长，故需啮啃硬物磨牙。所以民间亦称其为耗子。对应子时，是因为此时最为活跃。

鼠鼠

1924年
1936年
1948年
1960年
1972年
1984年
1996年
2008年

十二生肖　173

牛

材质：宋锦
规格：69.5×46.5 cm

OX / OXEN

Material: Song brocade
Height 69.5 × width 46.5 cm

人类早期的岩画,都有野牛的画像。一般都是一完整牛体。中国古人简化之为一牛头，进而简化为牛，仅突出牛角、牛耳。牛头和身体仅用一竖代表,表现了高超的抽象造型能力。

1925年
1937年
1949年
1961年
1973年
1985年
1997年
2009年

牛 牛 牛

十二生肖　175

虎　　　　　　　　　　TIGER

材质：宋锦　　　　　　　Material: Song brocade
规格：69.5×46.5 cm　　　Height 69.5× width 46.5 cm

虎的象形夸张了它的利齿，这已经是有强烈主观感受的写意了。大量与虎有关的字都联系着凶残。中国人的特点是怕什么便敬什么，所以青龙白虎同为瑞兽。虎对应寅时，大概与它夜间猎食的习性

1926年
1938年
1950年
1962年
1974年
1986年
1998年
2010年

要乃愛馬虎

兔　　　　　　　　HARE

材质：宋锦　　　　　　Material: Song brocade
规格：69.5×46.5 cm　　Height 69.5× width 46.5 cm

甲骨文兔，張嘴、短腿、長耳、短尾，造型很溫順。後逐漸演化，僅剩一點代兔尾，以區別於兔。兔溫馴且性別難辨，所以明清時代指男寵。老北京稱妓女為雞，男妓叫"兔"、"兔兔爺"，也叫相(xiang)公。兔与卯时相對，大概与官吏卯時上朝點名(點卯)有關。

1927年
1939年
1951年
1963年
1975年
1987年
1999年
2011年

兔兔兔兔

十二生肖

龙 DRAGON

材质：宋锦
规格：69.5×46.5 cm

Material: Song brocade
Height 69.5 × width 46.5 cm

甲骨文秀秀告诉了我们龙的原型，是一條大蟒蛇頭上多了"干"，有人釋為角，有人釋為辛，一種刑具，皆不通。對比䲪鳳，也是在鳥上加"干"，說明這就是祭司戴的頭飾，以表示神性。可參看紅山文化之C形龍，公認5000年前最早的玉龍，其頭上並非角或刑具，而是飄揚的頭飾。

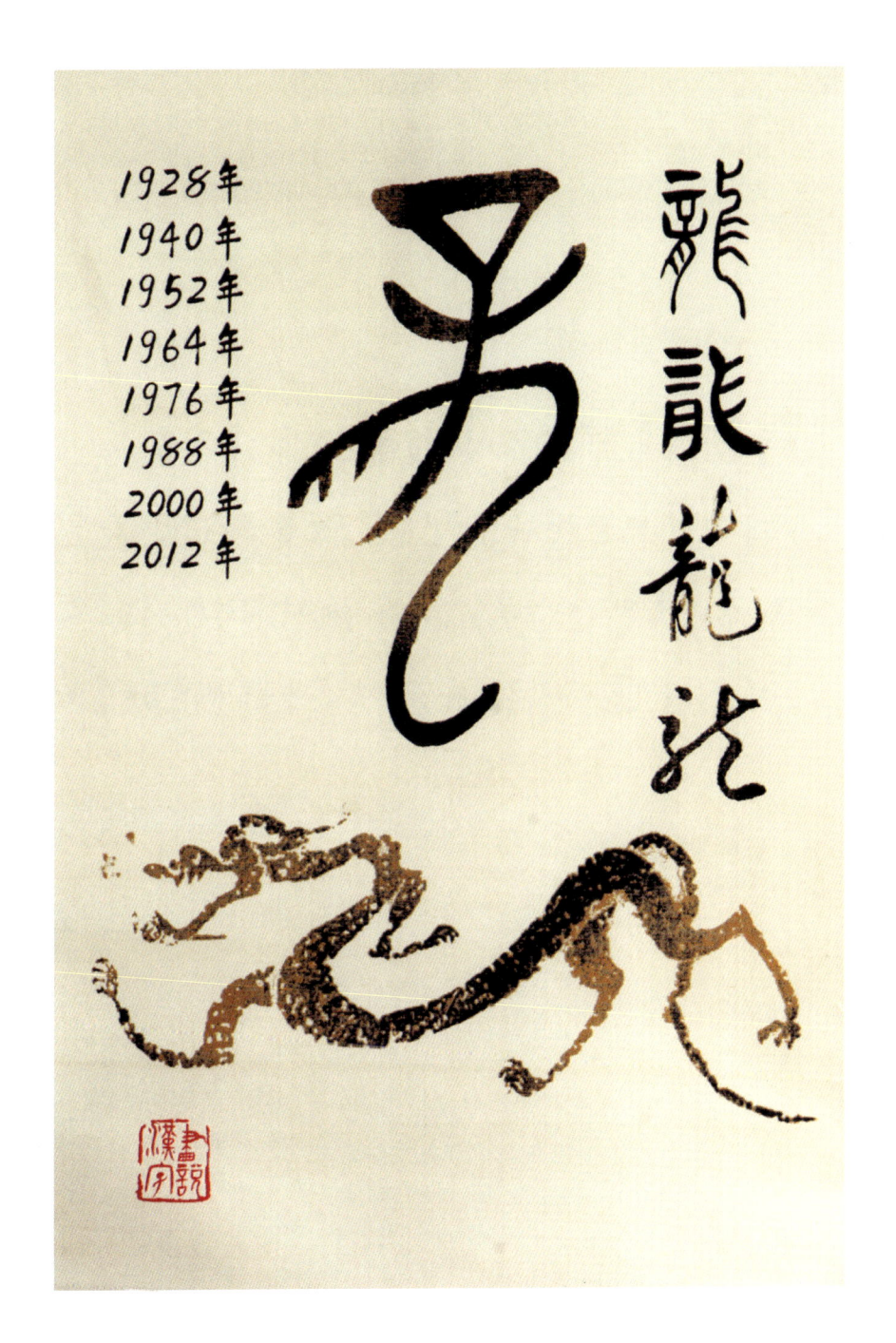

1928年
1940年
1952年
1964年
1976年
1988年
2000年
2012年

十二生肖

蛇　　　　　　　　SNAKE

材质：宋锦　　　　　Material: Song brocade
规格：69.5×46.5 cm　Height 69.5× width 46.5 cm

甲骨文也就是蛇的象形。後来这个字演变为蠶、虫。它的原型也也是蛇的象型。它就是蛇，後人在它旁加虫，表示毒蛇这一概念。古人怕蛇，故神化之，不僅演为龙图腾，还将人类始祖伏羲女娲想像为人首蛇身。

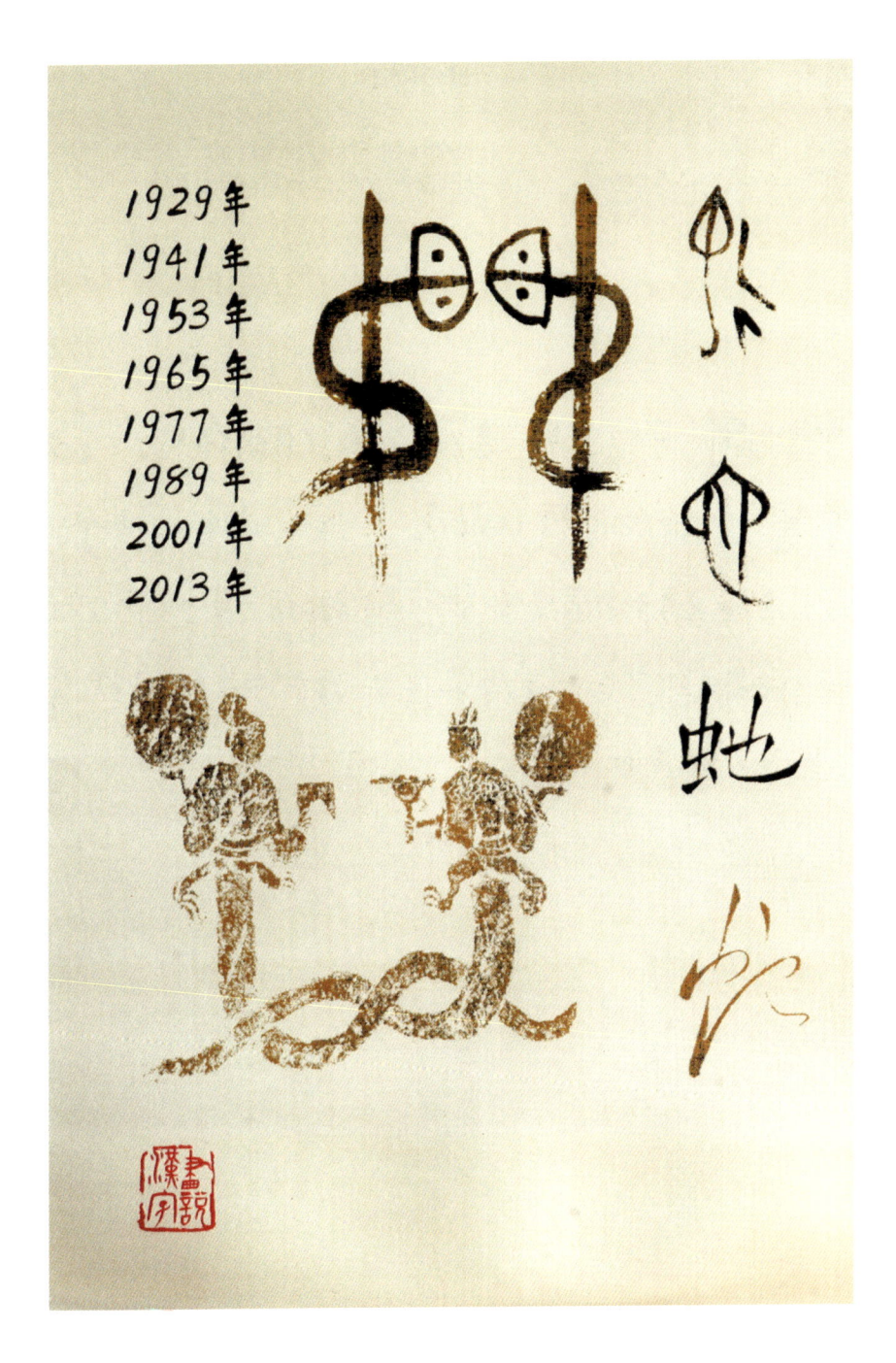

1929年
1941年
1953年
1965年
1977年
1989年
2001年
2013年

十二生肖

马　　　　　　　　　HORSE

材质：宋锦
规格：69.5×46.5 cm

Material: Song brocade
Height 69.5× width 46.5 cm

甲骨文夸张马鬃、马蹄，以表现马的神骏。金文逐渐向符号化发展。马作为部首的汉字有很多，许多良马专用的字如骢、骕骦现已基本不用，但反映了中国对良马的喜爱和渴望。汉武帝甚至为了抢夺名马而不惜发动战争。

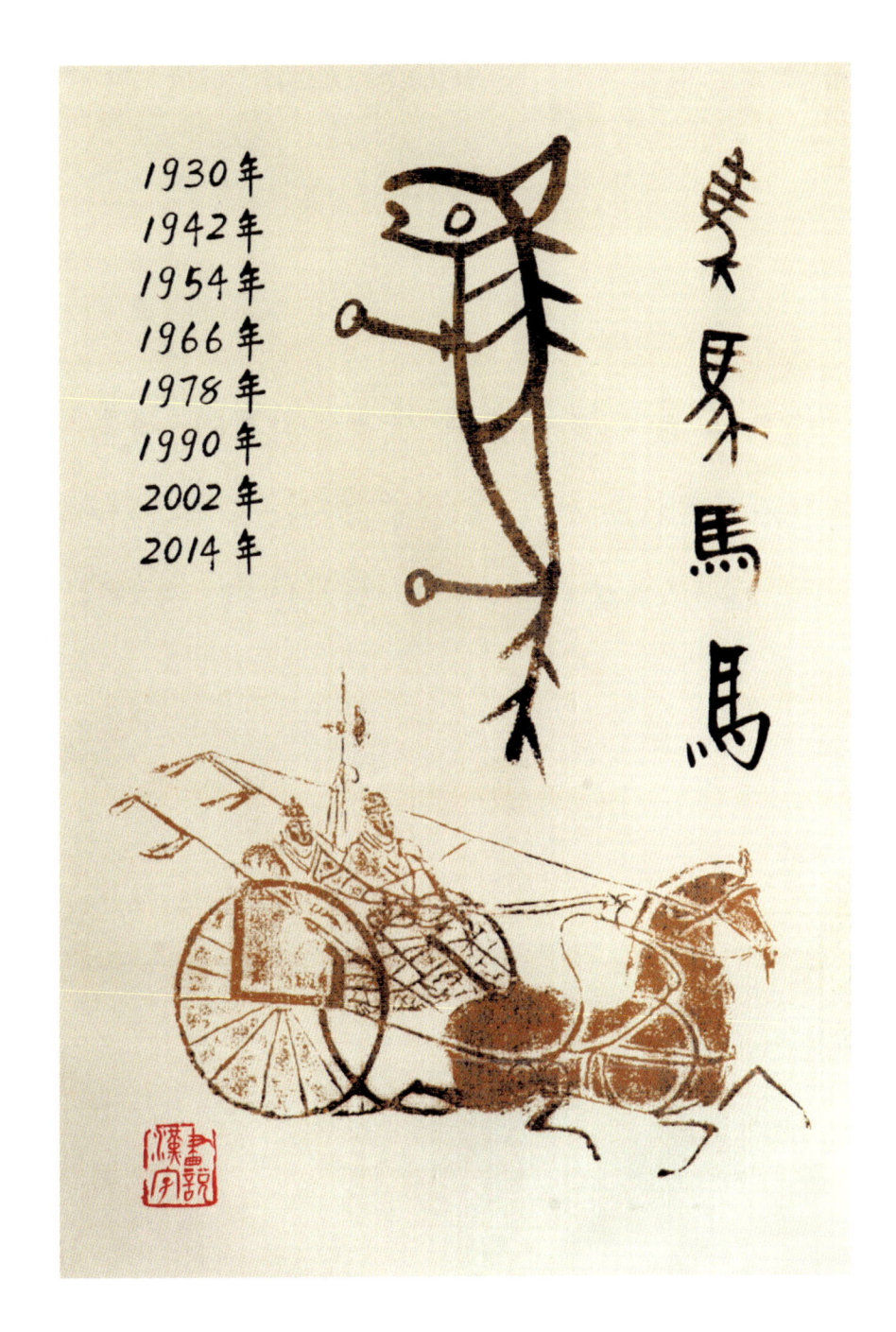

1930年
1942年
1954年
1966年
1978年
1990年
2002年
2014年

十二生肖　185

羊　　　　　　　　　SHEEP / GOAT

材质：宋锦　　　　　　Material: Song brocade
规格：69.5×46.5 cm　　Height 69.5× width 46.5 cm

甲骨文是羊颠的象形，弯曲的角有别于牛角。两鼻孔在鼻尖形成V形。金文夸张了羊角，十分匀称美观。羊是古人祭祀的太牲，因此通祥。是十分吉祥的汉字。

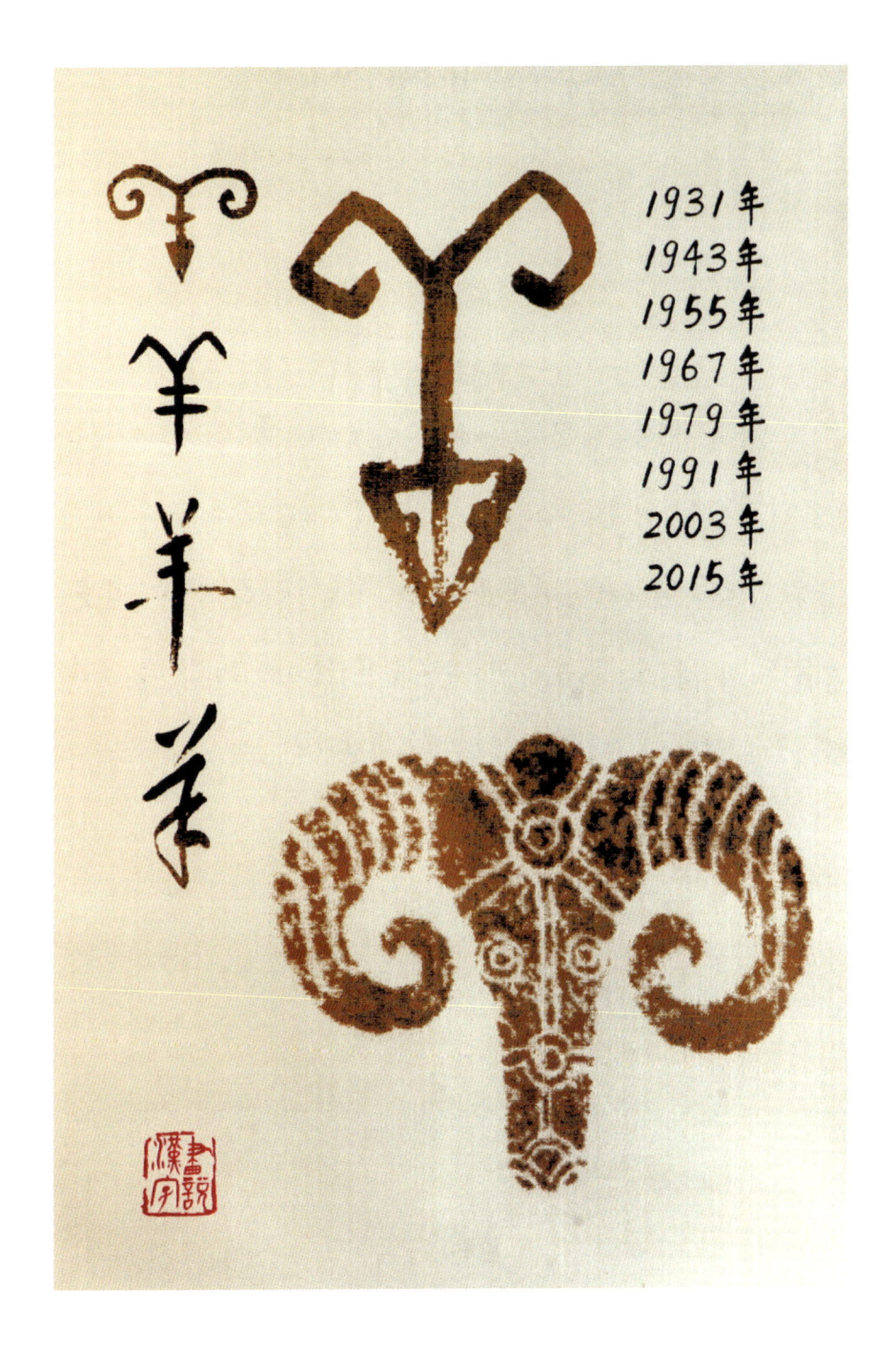

1931年
1943年
1955年
1967年
1979年
1991年
2003年
2015年

十二生肖

猴　　　　　　　　　　MONKEY

材质：宋锦　　　　　　　Material: Song brocade
规格：69.5×46.5 cm　　 Height 69.5× width 46.5 cm

這是猴的古字夒（náo），《說文》：夒，貪獸也，一曰母猴。就是一只猴子的象形。此字已被同音同意的"猱"（náo）所取代。猴《說文》：猴，夒也。侯的本意是箭到靶倒的箭靶吧，引申為分封這地的諸侯，犬旁的猴大概指猴是人類的遠親吧。

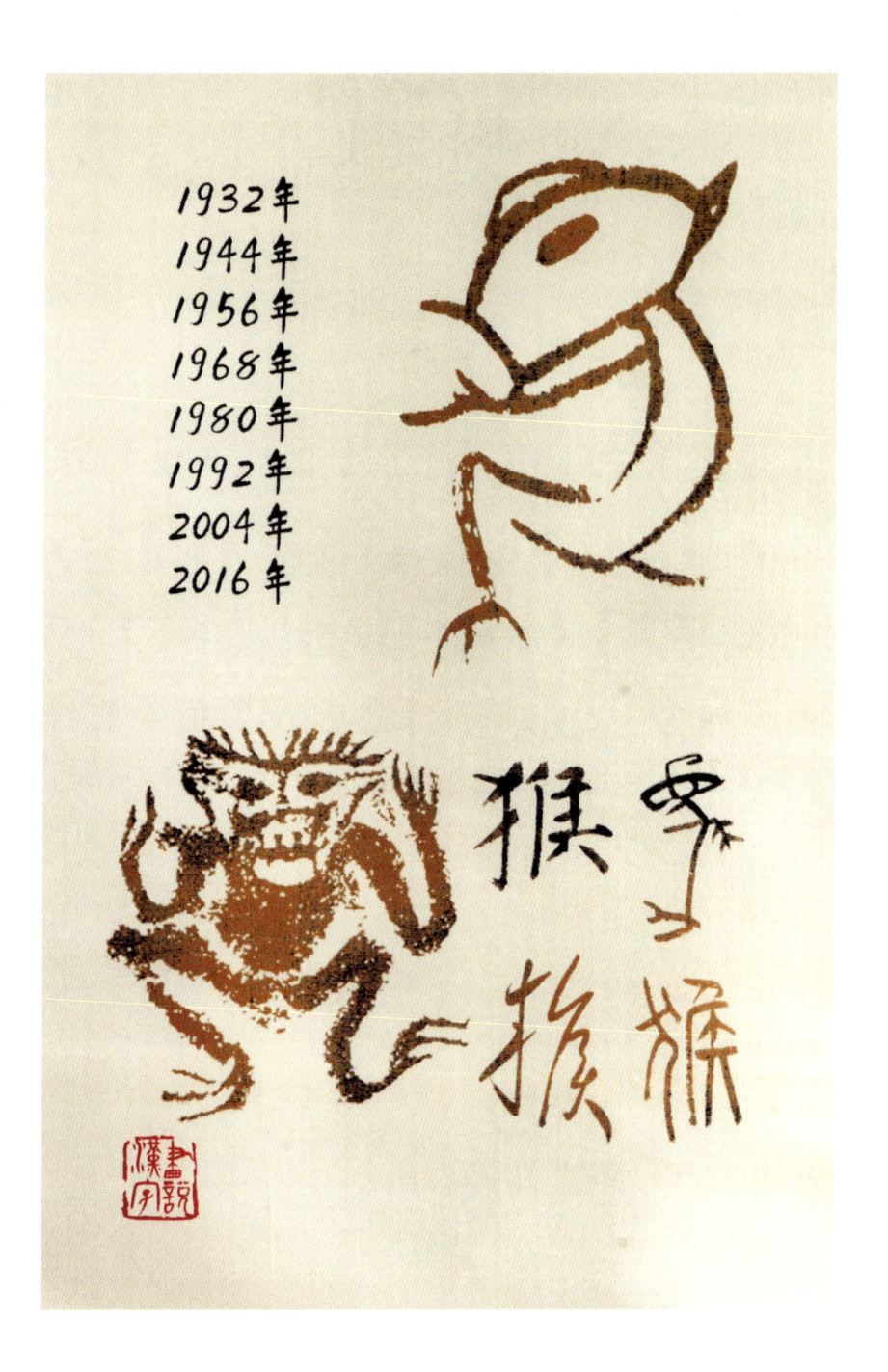

1932年
1944年
1956年
1968年
1980年
1992年
2004年
2016年

猴

十二生肖

鸡

ROOSTER / CHICKEN / COCK / HEN

材质：宋锦
规格：69.5×46.5 cm

Material: Song brocade
Height 69.5 × width 46.5 cm

鷄 這是甲骨文的另一種寫法，在一隻仰天打鳴的鳥旁，加了一個會意的"奚"，奚的原意是手抓捆綁著的奴隸，合起來意为抓來捆綁馴養的大鳥。《說文》：雞，知時畜也。說明古人最重視的是雞的報時功能

雞雞鷄

1933年
1945年
1957年
1969年
1981年
1993年
2005年
2017年

十二生肖

狗   DOG / CANINE

材质：宋锦
规格：69.5 × 46.5 cm

Material: Song brocade
Height 69.5 × width 46.5 cm

甲骨文丈犬是狗的象形。孔子曰：视犬之字如画狗也。的确如此，金文也就是狗的象形图画。小篆犬渐失其形，犬则全失象形。犬旁加句为狗。句句，指话语一句连着一句的转折，此处代狗吠。

天狗狐狗

1934年
1946年
1958年
1970年
1982年
1994年
2006年
2018年

十二生肖

猪 PIG / HOG / SWINE

材质：宋锦
规格：69.5 × 46.5 cm

Material: Song brocade
Height 69.5 × width 46.5 cm

甲骨文豕(shǐ)是一头肥猪的象形。猪是先民定居后最重要的财产，是安定、富足的象徵。所以家从宀房屋从豕，猪豬是後造的形聲字。甲骨文"尞"者是木柴著火的形狀，表示部落生火煮食聚眾漫談。火堆熊，煮肉漫談，其樂融也。

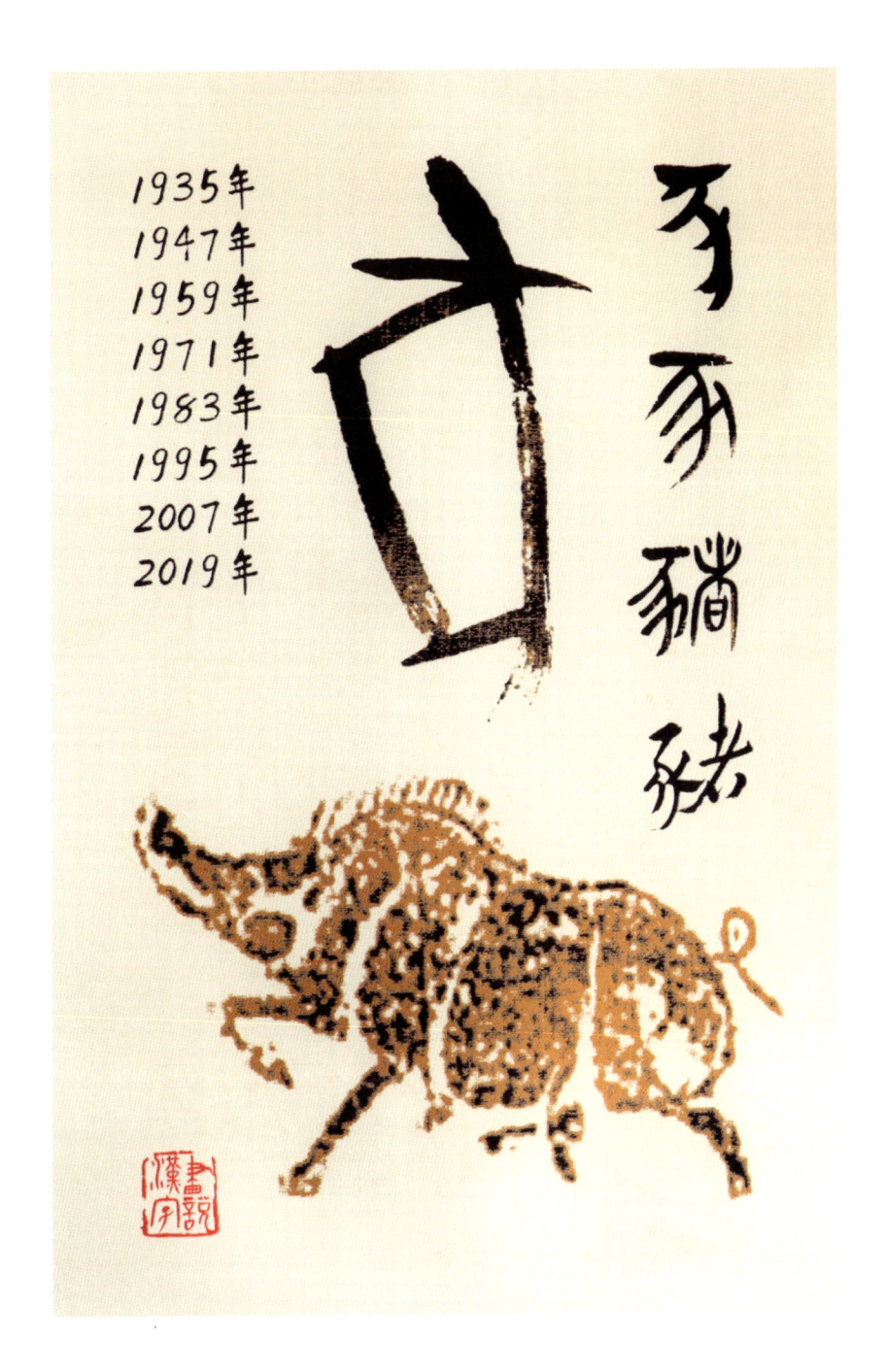

1935年
1947年
1959年
1971年
1983年
1995年
2007年
2019年

亥豕猪豨

十二生肖　195

吉祥字
AUSPICIOUS WORDS

福   BLESSING

材质：宋锦
规格：150×130 cm

Material: Song brocade
Height 150× width 130 cm

甲骨文福是雙手捧酒壇向神敬獻. 糧有餘才可釀酒. 所以福是富裕. 恭敬獻祭. 福是感恩. 祭祀後飲酒歡慶. 福是分享. 有酒, 有祭台. 因此福不可倒掛.

福

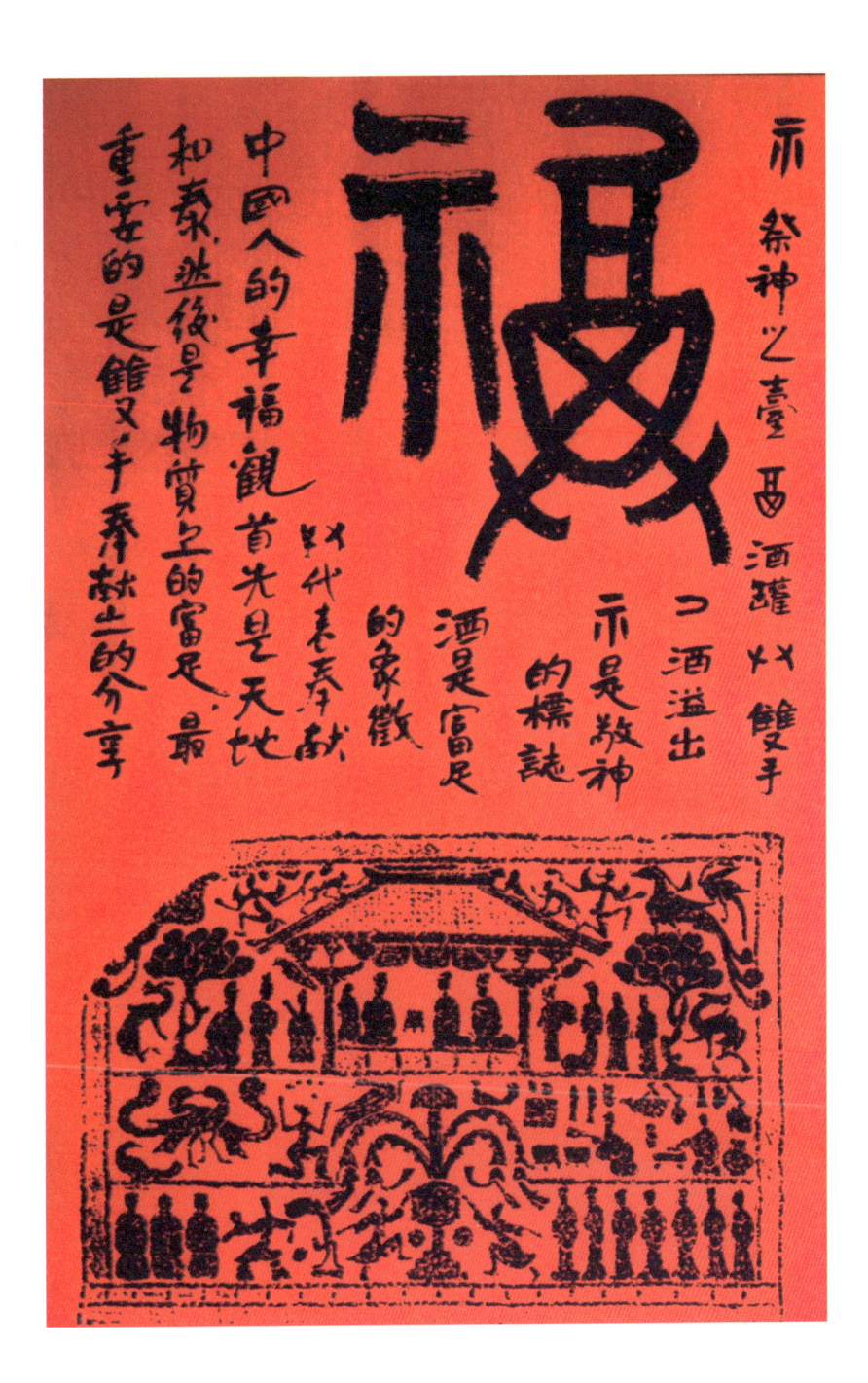

示 祭神之臺 畐 酒罐 廾 雙手
冂 酒溢出
示是敬神的標誌
酒是富足的象徵
以代表奉獻

中國人的幸福觀首先是天地和豢,然後是物質上的富足,最重要的是饍又手奉獻出的分享

吉祥字 199

禄   **PROSPERITY**

材质：宋锦
规格：150×130 cm

Material: Song brocade
Height 150× width 130 cm

甲骨文录，干是井架辘轳，曰是盛水容器，㣺是水。井代表农田，井水代表田地所产粮食。古代官员工资称为俸禄，俸指货币，禄指粮食。"示"指为官要敬天。"录"指官员收入取之于民，为官一任，造福一方。

示，祭台在此表示為官雲敬農

天地，雲用糖轎從井中汲水的情形；

神壽示為官害對天地負責汲取井水表示賦稅俸祿尤如井水取之於民，要取之有度取之有道

示代表的天地鬼

古代官吏的薪俸

祿指

寿　　　　　　　LONGEVITY

材质：宋锦　　　　Material: Song brocade
规格：150×130 cm　Height 150× width 130 cm

丬 扌披散头发的老人。古人束发，只有年长者方可披散头发。吕是神兮的变形，此处指大腿。曰口指口齿清晰。乂手指手脚灵便。寿是指充满智慧的健康老人。

夫 长髯老人状，意为年长 邑大脑
盘曲通透状 意为富有 智慧
千干的 形状 意为手脚 灵便
日口的形状 意为口齿 清晰

喜   HAPPINESS / BLISS

材质：宋锦　　　　　　　Material: Song brocade
规格：150×130 cm　　　Height 150× width 130 cm

甲骨文"喜"是鼓，代表慶典。"口"口代表歡笑。擊鼓歡笑，大喜。擊鼓表示人逢喜事一定宴分享，聚集慶祝，奔走相告，反映了農業社會的社會關素。

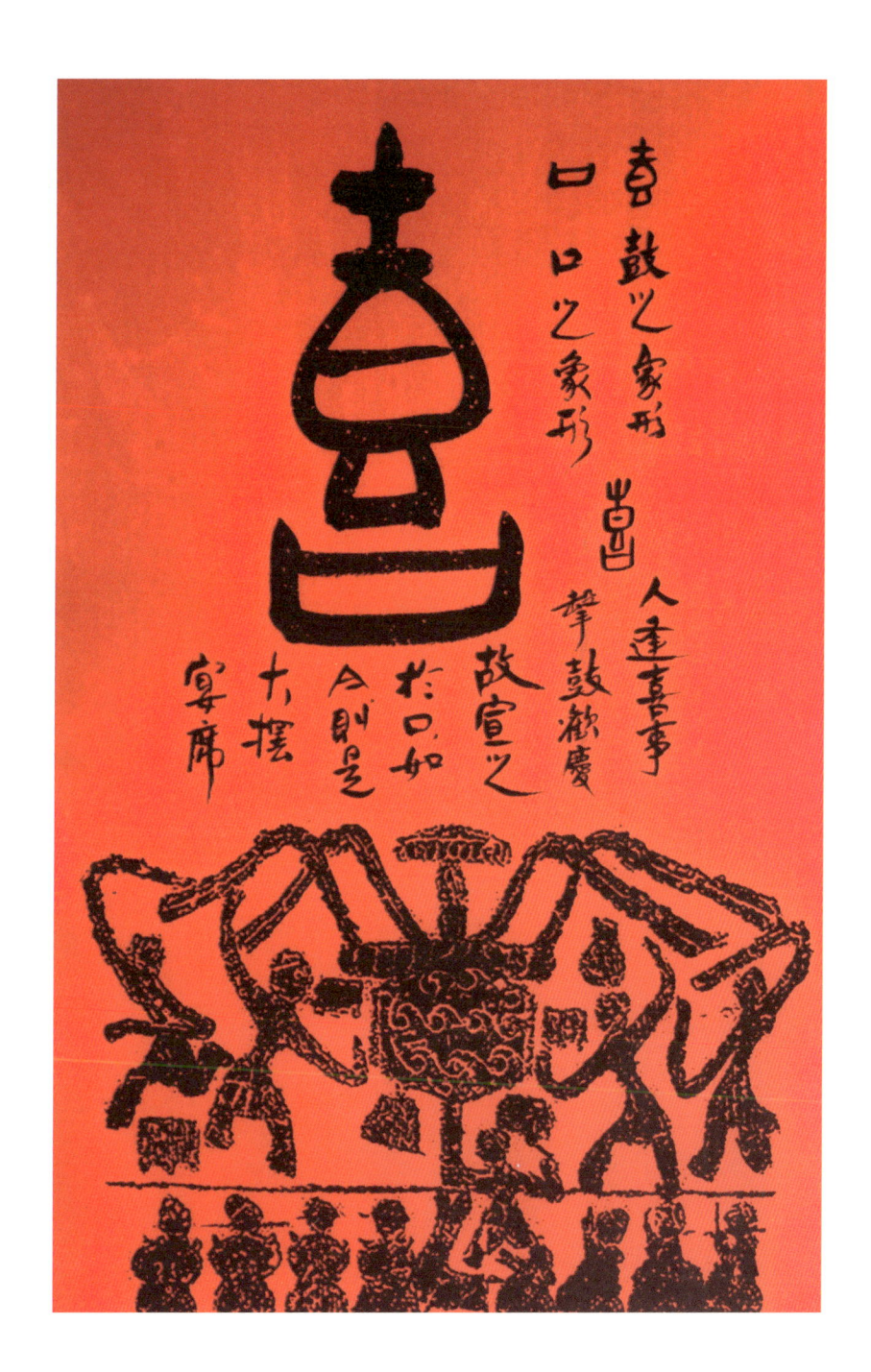

喜 鼓之象形
口 口之象形 䘗 人逢喜事
擊鼓歡慶
故宣之
於口如
合則是
大擺
宴席

龙　　　　　　　　DRAGON

材质：纸质　　　　　Material: paper
规格：69.5 × 46.5 cm　Height 69.5 × width 46.5 cm

傳說人類始祖伏羲、女媧人首龍（蛇）身，因此被称为龍祖。中國人因此自称龍的傳人。頭有角为公龍，雙角为龍，單角为蛟，无角为螭。龍在秦以後成为皇帝象徵。龍居東方，五行屬木，七因青色屬木，故称为青龍。

龍

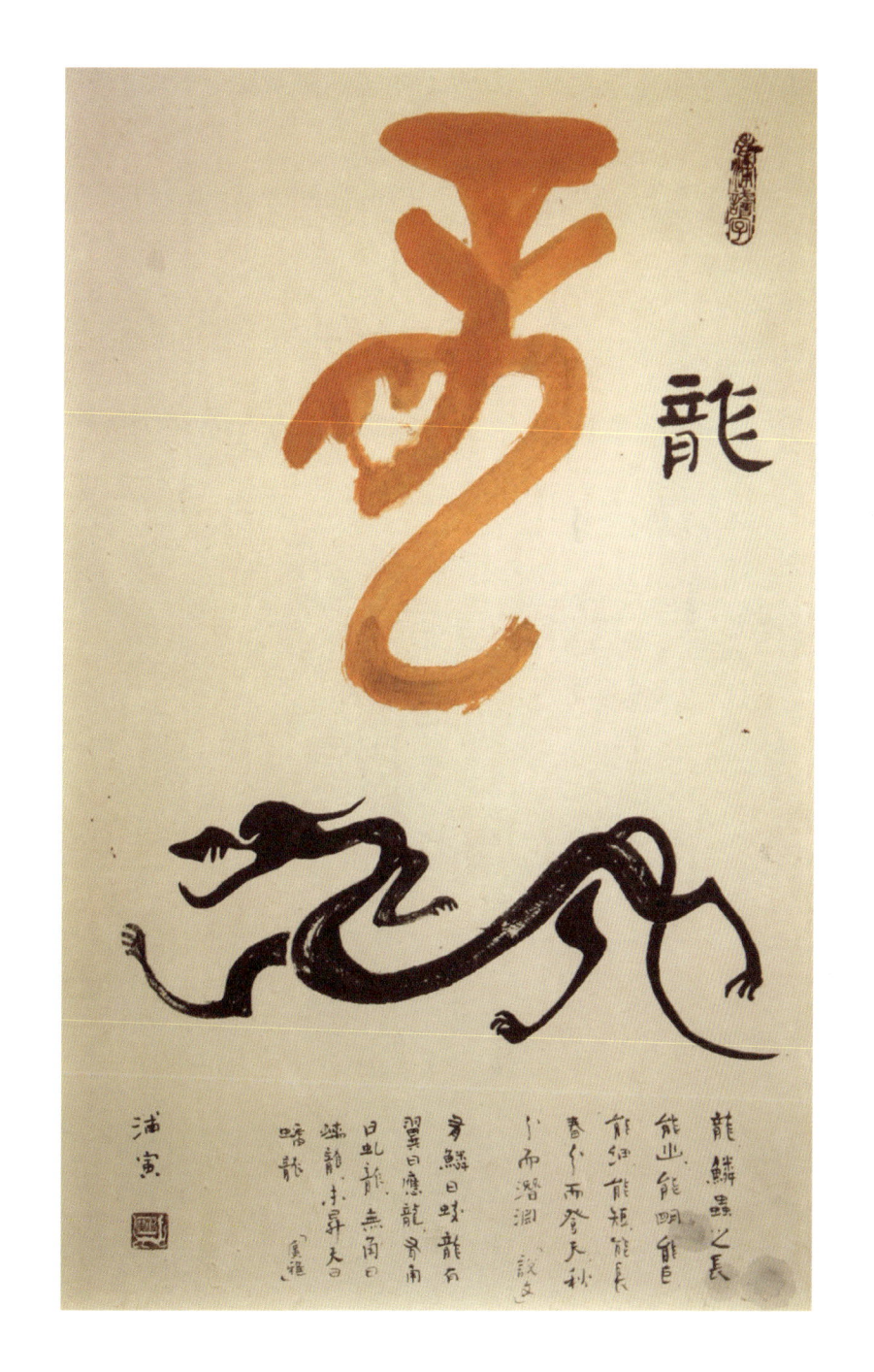

龍鱗蟲之長
能幽能明能細
能巨能短能長
春分而登天秋
分而潛淵（說文）

身無日蛟龍有
翼曰應龍骨甬
曰虬龍無角曰
螭龍未昇天曰
蟠龍（廣雅）

溥寅

凤   PHOENIX

材质：纸质
规格：69.5 × 46.5 cm

Material: paper
Height 69.5 × width 46.5 cm

凤，是中国古老传说的百鸟之王。雄的为凤雌的为凰，通称凤。是吉祥的象征，也是皇后的代称，与龙、麒麟、龟一起合称四瑞兽。凤分五种：赤色的朱雀、青色的青鸾、黄色的鹓鶵、白色的鸿鹄、紫色的鸑鷟。

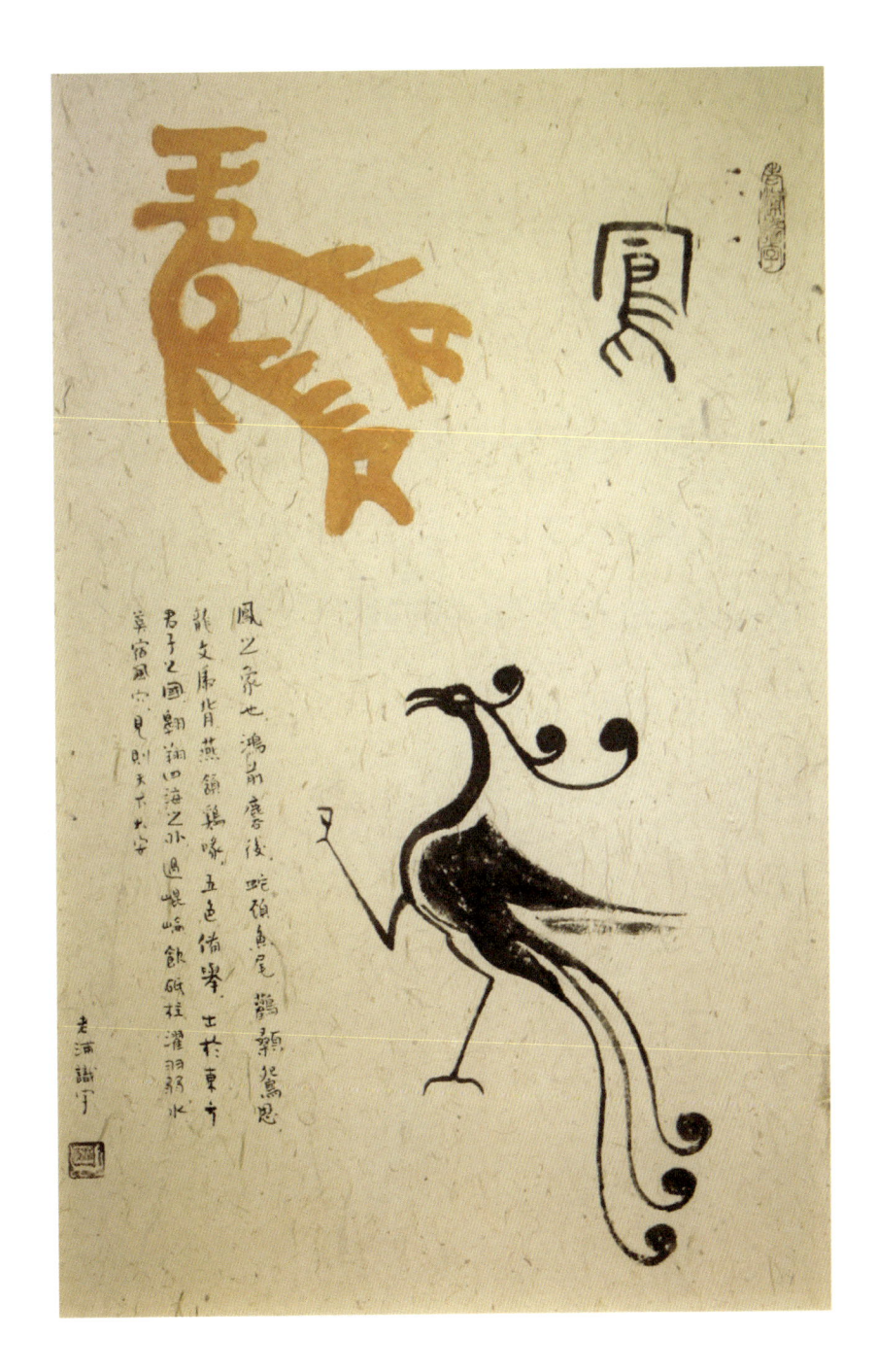

鳳之象也，鴻前麐後，蛇頸魚尾，鸛顙鴛思，龍文虎背，燕頷雞喙，五色備舉，出於東方君子之國，翱翔四海之外，過崑崙，飲砥柱，濯羽弱水，莫宿風穴，見則天下大安。

老涛谨书

虎　　　　　TIGER

材质：纸质
规格：69.5 × 46.5 cm

Material: paper
Height 69.5 × width 46.5 cm

虎是中国人尊崇的真实存在的动物。《风俗通义》云："虎者，阳物，百兽之长也，能执搏挫。"作为神兽，"云从龙，风从虎。"是战国颇代之神，西方的代表，西方属金，色白，故称白虎。

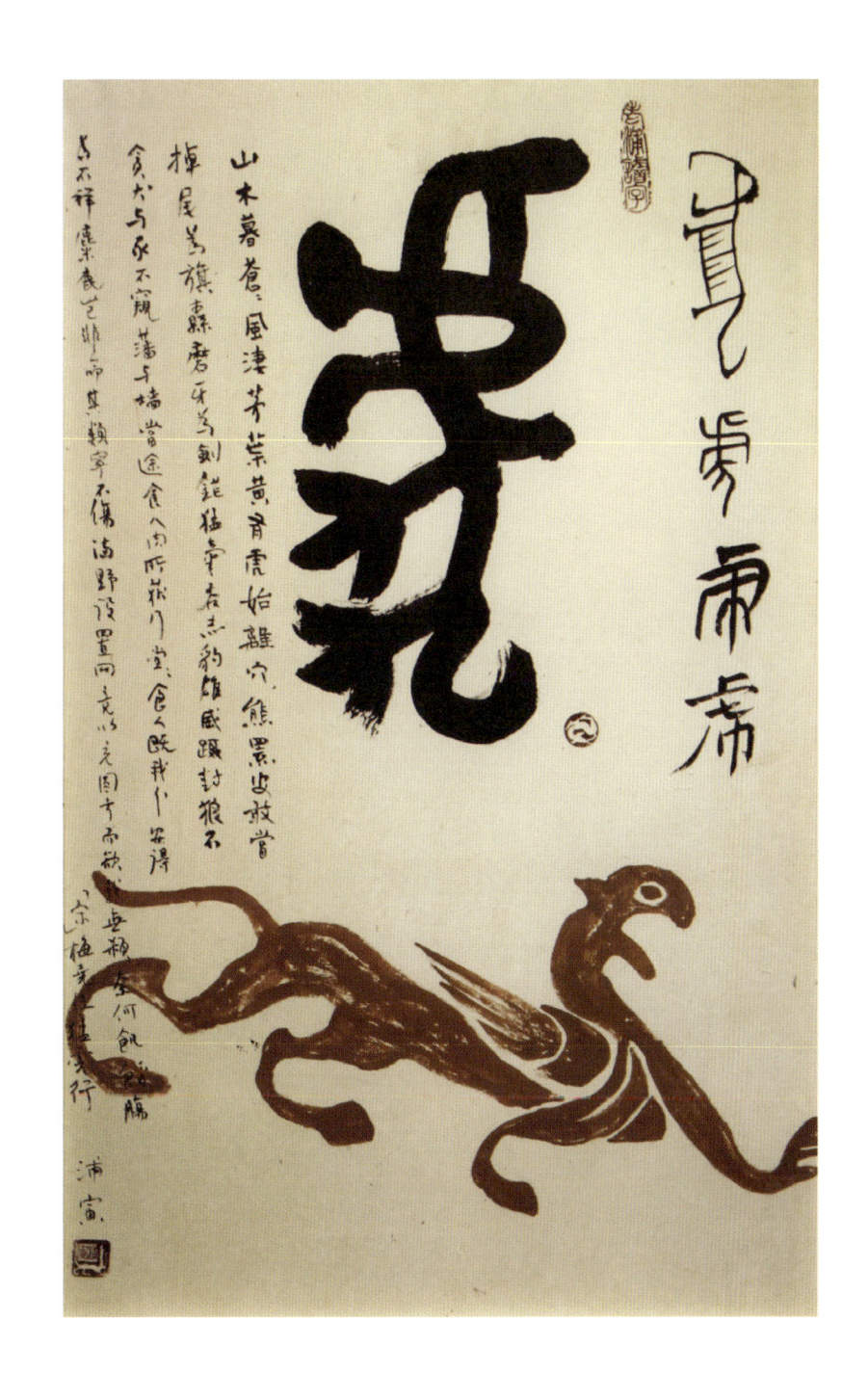

山木暮蒼，風淒芳葉黃肯霍始離穴，熊羆出故當揮尾為旗赤鼷磨牙為劍錐猛拿者志豹雄威蹴封狼不貪大与永不窺藩于墻甞途食人肉昕我仁安得馬不祥康羲芑邪命基賴寧不傷海野後置同竟火灾圉宁而畿戈些頼奎何飫砂臁宗伍亥 猩逶行

溥儒

飞 　　　　　　　　　　FLY

材质：纸质　　　　　　Material: paper
规格：69.5×46.5 cm　　Height 69.5 × width 46.5 cm

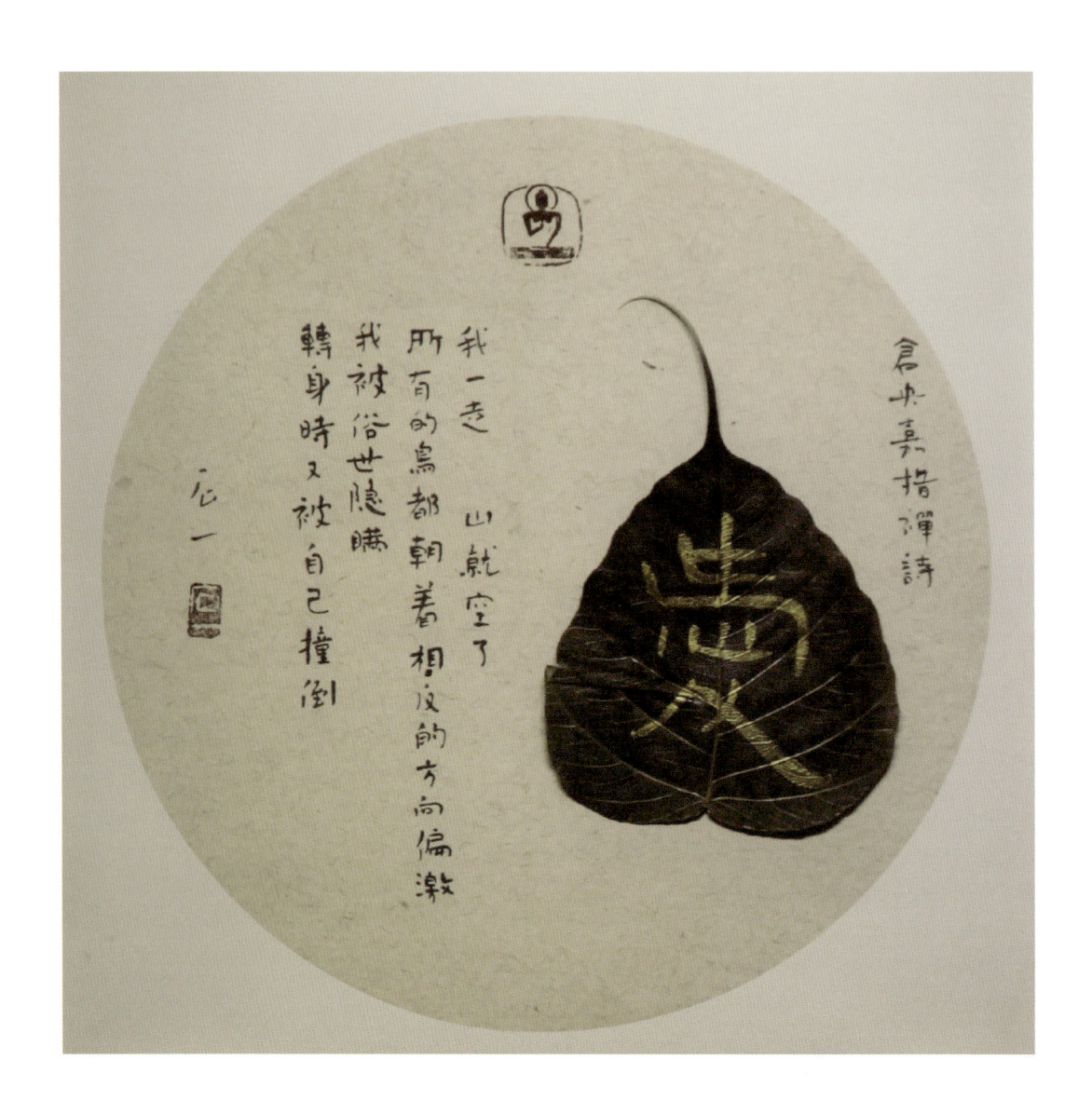

抄录仓央嘉措诗　　*Tsangyang Gyatso's poem*

材质：纸质 / 菩提树叶　　Material: paper / Bodhi leaf
规格：38 × 38 cm　　Height 38 × width 38 cm

用一朵蓮花商量我們的來世
再用一生的時間奔向對方
你穿過世事朝我走來
邁走的每一步都留下了一座空城
這時一支迷來世射出的毒箭命定了我
唯一的退路

倉央嘉措禪詩

抄录仓央嘉措诗

Tsangyang Gyatso's poem

材质：纸质 / 菩提树叶
规格：38×38 cm

Material: paper / Bodhi leaf
Height 38 × width 38 cm

抄录仓央嘉措诗

Tsangyang Gyatso's poem

材质：纸质 / 菩提树叶
规格：38 × 38 cm

Material: paper / Bodhi leaf
Height 38 × width 38 cm

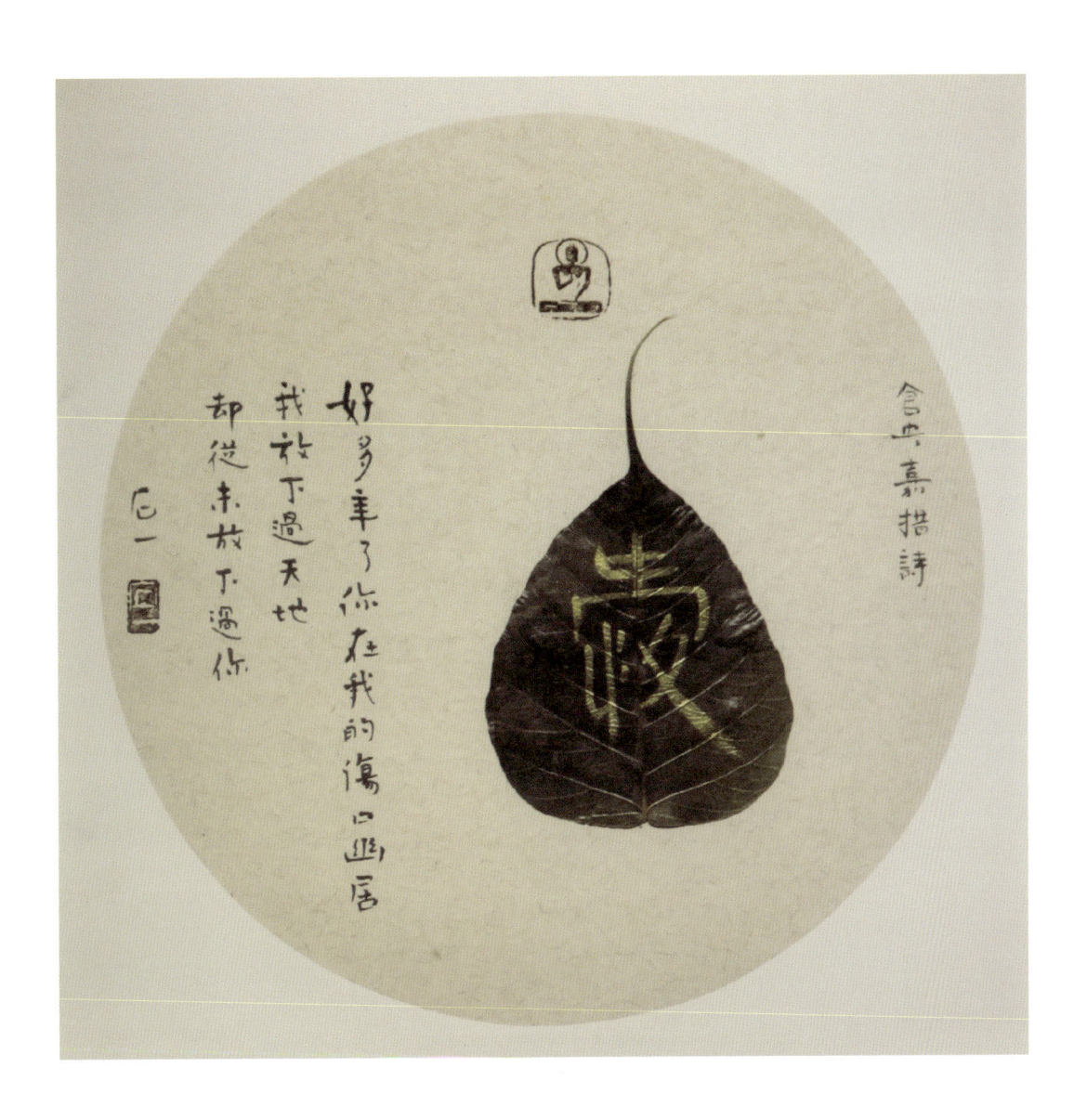

抄录仓央嘉措诗

材质：纸质 / 菩提树叶
规格：38 × 38 cm

Tsangyang Gyatso's poem

Material: paper / Bodhi leaf
Height 38 × width 38 cm

抄录尼采诗

Nietzsche's poem

材质：纸质 / 树皮
规格：38 × 38 cm

Material: paper / bark
Height 38 × width 38 cm

抄录尼采诗

Nietzsche's poem

材质：纸质 / 树皮
规格：38 × 38 cm

Material: paper / bark
Height 38 × width 38 cm

抄录尼采诗

Nietzsche's poem

材质：纸质 / 树皮
规格：38 × 38 cm

Material: paper / bark
Height 38 × width 38 cm

抄录尼采诗   *Nietzsche's poem*

材质：纸质 / 树皮　　　　Material: paper / bark
规格：38×38 cm　　　　　Height 38 × width 38 cm

图书在版编目(CIP)数据

画说汉字 / 浦寅著. -- 北京：社会科学文献出版社，2017.9
　　ISBN 978-7-5201-1283-3

　　Ⅰ.①画… Ⅱ.①浦… Ⅲ.①汉字－通俗读物 Ⅳ.①H12-49

中国版本图书馆CIP数据核字(2017)第202231号

画说汉字

著　　者 /	浦　寅
出 版 人 /	谢寿光
项目统筹 /	关晶焱
责任编辑 /	关晶焱　尤　雅
出　　版 /	社会科学文献出版社·独立编辑工作室 (010) 59367105 地址：北京市北三环中路甲29号院华龙大厦　邮编：100029 网址：www.ssap.com.cn
发　　行 /	市场营销中心 (010) 59367081　59367018
印　　装 /	北京盛通印刷股份有限公司
规　　格 /	开　本：787mm×1092mm 1/16 印　张：14　字　数：107千字
版　　次 /	2017年9月第1版　2017年9月第1次印刷
书　　号 /	ISBN 978-7-5201-1283-3
定　　价 /	58.00元

本书如有印装质量问题，请与读者服务中心 (010-59367028) 联系

▲ 版权所有　翻印必究